God bless the use
of this book!

JHBaumgartner

Lent, 1960

To
Aunt Marion and Uncle Dan
from Edith

Easter, 1960

meet the
TWELVE

meet the
TWELVE

by
John H. Baumgaertner

AUGSBURG PUBLISHING HOUSE
MINNEAPOLIS 15, MINNESOTA

MEET THE TWELVE
© 1960 Augsburg Publishing House
Library of Congress Catalog Card No. 60-6440

Manufactured in the United States of America

TO MY WIFE

*who in the full sharing of all our life
has brought a blessed and happy fulfillment.*

It is not good that the man should be alone;
I will make him a helper fit for him.

GENESIS 2:18

PREFACE

"Go therefore and make disciples of all nations . . ."
That was His last word, His great commission. We
are far from the mark today if we think of our rela-
tionship with Jesus Christ in terms of anything less
than full discipleship. He didn't say "Go and make
church-goers," or "Go and make congregation members." Of course His disciples of the twentieth century will go to church and they will be congregation
members. But they must become His disciples first
of all. And they must live their Christian life in terms
of a personal discipleship with their Lord and Redeemer.

Isn't it strange, then, that we know so little about
the twelve men who were the first disciples of Jesus?
The average church-going congregation member is
unable to name more than five or six of them. The
fact is that there are several among the Twelve of
whom there is almost nothing to be known. Most
Christians are not even aware of that. There are
others of whom we know a great deal. Too many of

Christ's disciples of the present day have not even made their acquaintance.

On the first twelve Sundays of 1959 the members of Capitol Drive Lutheran Church in Milwaukee, Wisconsin, were invited to "meet the Twelve" in a series of sermons to which the congregation and many others in the community responded in a manner which provided convincing evidence that people do want to make the acquaintance of the men whom Jesus gathered about Himself and upon whom He laid the burden of duty to make disciples in all the world. So many who heard the messages or missed one or two of the series requested copies that it was decided to publish them in book form and make them generally available.

The purpose of this volume is stated in the title, "Meet the Twelve." There is no attempt here to provide an annotated and documented source book. Such books exist and they have been immensely helpful in the preparation of these introductions to the disciples of Jesus. Unfortunately, though they don't deserve that kind of fate, they are likely to appear far too pedantic to the inquirer who is not theologically trained, and so remain unread. Nor is it their purpose, as it is the purpose of this book, to establish, by means of varied applications, a real link between the discipleship of the first century and that of today.

Here, then, is a modest and humble attempt, without pretense or affectation, to bridge a gap between the centuries and bring together the twelve disciples of Jesus and His followers of the present day. In more ways than one, it is terribly important that those who live and move within the circle of His friends learn to know each other better. Only God knows how fully our lack of understanding of and for each other has contributed to a divided church.

We need to know and understand the Twelve. And this, above all, is important. Inevitably a closer acquaintance with the Twelve will draw us from the fringes of the circle to Him who is its heart and center.

There at the heart and center, from the lips of Him who loved us and gave Himself for us, we hear words like these:

"If you continue in My word, you are truly My disciples, and you will know the truth, and the truth will make you free."

"My sheep hear My voice, and I know them, and they follow Me; and I give them eternal life, and they shall never perish."

JOHN H. BAUMGAERTNER

Pentecost, 1959

CONTENTS

Andrew is said to have been crucified on an X-shaped cross.

Andrew

The next day again John was standing with two of his disciples; and he looked at Jesus as he walked, and said, "Behold, the Lamb of God!" The two disciples heard him say this, and they followed Jesus. Jesus turned, and saw them following, and said to them, "What do you seek?" And they said to him, "Rabbi (which means teacher), where are you staying?" He said to them, "Come and see." They came and saw where he was staying; and they stayed with him that day, for it was about the tenth hour. One of the two who heard John speak, and followed him, was Andrew, Simon Peter's brother. He first found his brother Simon, and said to him, "We have found the Messiah" (which means Christ). He brought him to Jesus.

JOHN 1:35-42a

ANDREW

*Always helpful, often
far more than he knew.*

THE mighty Mississippi begins with the bubbling of a little spring somewhere in Minnesota. Vast areas of Holland have been covered by floods that began with a break in the dikes no larger than your hand. When we trace great events, great movements, great organizations and often great men to their beginnings we find them humble and small.

What an insignificant event it was in the history of the world, the first meeting of Jesus of Nazareth with the little group of humble men who became His disciples! One of them was Andrew, a fisherman, a disciple of John the Baptist. Thrilled by the voice and the personality of the gaunt and fiery prophet who had come out of the wilderness, won by the message of repentance that he preached, Andrew was waiting, waiting with an eager and a throbbing heart, for that greater Prophet of whom the Baptist spoke.

Then, one day, a new figure quietly approached the edge of the crowd that was listening to the Baptist, and suddenly John, his face burning with a great light, cried out to them all, "Behold, the Lamb of God, who takes away the sin of the world!" Andrew turned, and his eyes met the eyes of Jesus, and in that moment was established a kinship that was to last through all eternity.

Without a word Jesus left the crowd and Andrew, with an unnamed companion, followed Him, drawn by some deep, strange, inner compulsion. Jesus, perceiving that He was being followed, turned and looked at them. "What do you seek?" He said. And they said to Him, "Rabbi, where are you staying?" The question gave little sense, but Jesus smiled and said, "Come and see." So they went with Him to the cheap lodging house where He was staying and spent the day with Him. That day Andrew "found a new world" and entered upon a new life. He became the first-called of the Twelve, a faithful, affectionate, devoted Helper of Christ and the world that Christ had come to save. He was never the spectacular disciple. But in his own quiet, unassuming way, he was always bringing others to Jesus. The whole story of his life, as it is sketched out for us in the inspired narrative, resolves around three incidents, in each of which he brings someone to Jesus.

First it was Peter, his brother.—Andrew found Jesus, followed Him to His dwelling-place, stayed with Him for a day. And when the stars came out against the Judean night, and it was time to tear himself away, Andrew said: "I'm so glad you let me come. Now I will go and tell Peter." And off he went, back

to his own lodgings, and breathlessly he said to
Simon Peter, "We have found the Messiah!" The
story continues, in the very next sentence, "He
brought him to Jesus." It was all very simple. Nothing remarkable about it at all. A man finds the
Savior. He goes and tells his brother and brings him
to Jesus.

It wasn't simple at all. It was *most* remarkable, this
confession of faith on the part of Andrew and his
bringing of Peter to Jesus. To many of us today it is
self-evident that Jesus is the Son of God, the promised Messiah, the Savior of the world. We've been
hearing about it ever since we've been two or three
years old, ever since we've been old enough to be
told the meaning of Christmas. How different it must
have been for Andrew, suddenly to have the realiza-
tion burst upon him, suddenly to make the overwhelming discovery, that the promised Messiah was
standing there before him, He of whom the prophets
had spoken, He for whom Israel had been waiting
for two thousand years, the Seed of Abraham, the
Sun of Righteousness, the Prince of Peace, the Desire
of Nations, the Dayspring from on high. Millions
have believed in the centuries since, millions of every
nation and tribe and kindred and people and tongue;
they, too, found in Jesus of Nazareth the Messiah,
the Christ of God, the Redeemer of the world. But
Andrew was the first of them all, Andrew, humble
fisherman of Galilee, Andrew, a sailor of the Galilean
lakes.

It was a discovery, as we heard before, that simply had to be shared, and so Andrew brought Simon Peter to Jesus. And Simon was his *brother!* Did you know that Simon and Andrew were brothers? Did you know that they were boys together near the sandy shores of the Sea of Galilee? Did you know that, as brothers, they were partners in the fishing business? As often happens, they were brothers who were not at all alike. They were almost opposites in personality and temperament. Peter was as impetuous as Andrew was quiet and reserved. While Peter sought the limelight, Andrew kept himself in the background. And while Peter was the born leader, headstrong, determined, sure of himself, Andrew was the perfect follower and helper. Peter wasn't the sort of man whom others could easily command. He was used to having his own way and going where he pleased.

That's exactly what makes this little incident, of such far-reaching consequence for the history of the church, all the more remarkable. Andrew had every reason to expect his big gruff brother to say: "Well, so you've found the Messiah! You, of all people, my quiet little brother, you've found the Messiah, found Him in a crowd at the river bank, and in a dismal rooming house! Andrew, you're out of your mind!" Andrew might well have expected that, and maybe it's exactly what happened. We don't know. We do know that he went to his brother, Peter, spoke to him with a joy in his voice and a fervor in his soul that could not be denied, and brought him to Jesus. Before long Peter was the great one among the Twelve, their leader, their spokesman, and Andrew had to practice what someone has aptly called "the talents of the second fiddle." Andrew was perfectly willing to be just himself and quietly serve and do the best he could and keep on bringing others to Jesus. Perhaps he never converted three thousand with a single sermon, as Peter did on Pentecost, but wasn't it enough to have brought Peter, who did the preaching?

It was a broken, discouraged, unspectacular, unsuccessful preacher who gained for the church one day a boy by the name of David; David Livingstone it was, who later brought the light of the Gospel to darkest Africa. Andrew went and got his brother, and his brother became the leader of them all.

Remember this, too. As the first Christian worker, Andrew began in the most difficult place of all, in his own home, with his own brother, with a brother who wasn't the kind of man who could easily be told what to do. Today—what about today? Have we the courage to begin with a brother, a wife or husband, a son or daughter, a father or mother? Have we dared to speak to those in our own home, within the circle of our close relations, about life and death, about God and eternity, about the Savior and His Church, about heaven and hell? Isn't it, for many of us, the most unlikely place in the world? Some of us would rather give a hundred dollars to foreign missions than to talk to a brother or sister about the eternal destiny of the immortal soul. Isn't it about time that we follow the example of Andrew, who, with a heaven-born enthusiasm, approached his boisterous brother and won him for the cause?

There came a day, later on, when the people were hungry, five thousand of them and more in a desert place, and they had no food. The disciples had a practical solution for that problem. "Send them away," they said. But Jesus said, "They don't need to go away. Why don't you feed them? How much food have you? Go and see!" Again it was Andrew who came forward, always the helpful disciple. Here is a boy, he reported, who brought his lunch. Five barley loaves and two fishes—a handful of buns and a couple of sardines, not nearly as much as one of our acolytes would take to a picnic. Andrew himself wasn't quite sure how that would help, but it was all the food he could find and so he brought the boy and his lunch basket to Jesus and he knew that Jesus somehow would do the rest. That's exactly what happened. Jesus fed the whole crowd with that boy's lunch. He took what a child had to offer, little as it was, and did wonders with it. And it was Andrew who had brought him to Jesus. Andrew was always helping, often far better than he knew.

Again we learn from him lessons for our own discipleship. How often have *we* said with Andrew, "There is a boy here," and have done something about it? Andrew discovered something that we so often fail to see: the hidden resources of a child. "There is a boy here," the father ought to say to himself, as he looks around the living room in his own home, "there is a boy here, adopting my traits of character, learning to walk in my ways, beginning to live the kind of life that I am holding before him, catching my point of view, my manner of speech, my attitude toward God and religion, my interpretation of life," and the father ought to bring that boy to his Savior. "There is a boy here," the Sunday school teacher ought to remind herself, as she faces her sometimes restless and unruly class, "there is a boy here who will soon be a man. I must help him, teach him, guide him, pray for him, lead him to the gates of the Kingdom." Paul of Tarsus, Martin Luther, all the great heroes and leaders of Christ's Church, were once restless boys. The great men of the future are boys today, and today it lies within our power to point them toward the higher things of life. The church of tomorrow will march on the feet of the boys and girls of today. Believe me, we pastors value, far more highly than we can tell you, the help of those within the church and community who are active in youth work. I like to think of them as belonging to a sort of Brotherhood of St. Andrew.

Finally, Andrew introduced a group of strangers to Christ. They were Greeks, "foreigners" to the Jews, who had heard about this prophet of Galilee and wanted to meet Him. They went first to Philip, and said: "Sir, we wish to see Jesus." Philip wasn't so sure it was a good idea. After all, these people were Gentiles, outlanders. And so he talked it over with Andrew. Andrew was perfectly willing to admit these "foreigners" into the presence of Christ. He knew that God is no respecter of persons, of nation or of color. Was he thinking of the Wise Men, the first representatives of the Gentile world to worship the new-born Christ? Was he looking forward to the day of a world-wide Christian church? Was he waiting for the time when the Master would be sending them forth "into all the world?" We don't know. We do know that he welcomed the Greeks and brought them to Jesus. In a sense he was the first foreign missionary of the Christian church. I wonder what he would think of the cold unconcern with which so many of us contemplate the pagan world today, how little we really care about the cause of missions, how little we are doing for the unsaved in the world today. If Andrew were to visit us today, he might have some questions to ask about our mission offerings.

One thing would please him, I know. It would please him to see the visitors who come to the services of worship, the people who, by their very presence in the house of God, are saying, "We wish to see Jesus." It would please him to see a corps of friendly ushers, cheerfully and warmly extending greetings, helping visitors to find a place within the church, a kind of fellowship of St. Andrew, doing what he would be doing if he were here today. It would please him even more if all of us, every Sunday, every time we come to church, would, by the cordial warmth of our welcome to others and the friendliness of our hospitality bring them a practical demonstration of Christian love, bring them closer, closer perhaps than they have ever been before, to the loving heart of Jesus.

That's all we know, from the Bible itself, about Andrew. Legend and tradition, some of it sublime, much of it ridiculous, continue his story until his martyrdom, his death upon an X-shaped cross. There is a painting, by the great Murillo, of Andrew's martyrdom. At one side the artist added the figure of a little boy, his face turned away as if he could not bear the terrible sight, tears streaming down his cheeks, the boy of the barley loaves and the fishes.

After Pentecost the sailor of Galilee became a navigator of the seven seas, preaching the Gospel of the Kingdom wherever the winds would take him. But we remember him today as the humble, helpful disciple, as the church worker among the Twelve, willing always without selfishness, without vainglory, to serve.

It is said that St. Francis of Assisi had a disciple by the name of Juniper, of whom he said, "Oh, for a forest of such Junipers." Many a minister of today has said, "Let me have a church of Andrews—of simple, loving men, content to bring others to Jesus."

The three scallop shells represent the apostle's travels.

James Major

James the son of Zebedee and John the brother of James, whom he surnamed Boanerges, that is, sons of thunder.

MARK 3:17

JAMES MAJOR

One of that blessed group.

PORT WASHINGTON, Wisconsin, has its Smith
Brothers, and the Smith Brothers have a prospering fishing business. In a certain village on the
Sea of Galilee it was Zebedee and Company, and
this, too, was a prospering fishing business. I'm sure
that Zebedee was looking forward to the day when
it would be Zebedee and Sons, when the two fine
boys who were the pride of his life and the joy of
his heart would become his business partners. They
were born fishermen, James and his younger brother,
John, conditioned from boyhood to the sight and
sound and smell and feel of wind and wave, of boats
and sails with all their gear and rigging, of pitch and
tar and wood and ropes and nets and fish. This was
their life, and their livelihood. Even as tiny boys they
had lived along the seashore, digging their brown
toes into the sand, playing among the upturned
boats, teasing and envying the men as they mended
their nets and stretched them out for drying, shading
their eyes as they looked out to the sea, dreaming
of days of voyage and adventure.

Little did they know then that One would come to them some day, call them from their boats and their nets, and make them fishers of men. Little did they know that they would sail not only the Sea of Galilee, but the great vast Mediterranean, on voyages of adventure that would stir the hearts of men for a hundred generations!

It was a hard day for Zebedee when he saw them go. Lean and bronzed, strong and straight and true they were, just as he had hoped. And now they were leaving him, leaving his beloved fishing business, to follow the Prophet of Nazareth. There was no stopping them. After seeing the light in their eyes and hearing the fervor in their voices, he didn't even try. Zebedee was growing old. It wouldn't be much longer, anyway.

When Zebedee died, not long thereafter, his wife, Salome, mother of John the Baptist, became a disciple, too, and joined them in the company that followed Jesus. It is possible, though we are not perfectly sure, that Salome was the sister of Mary, the mother of Jesus. In that case James and John were cousins of the Lord. Cousins or not, they were united with Him by ties of love and fellowship infinitely above and beyond all human relationships.

Now it is James Major, the Silent Disciple, with whom we want to become acquainted. We call him James Major because there was another James among the Twelve, whom men call James Minor, or James the Less. We shall meet him later on.

There are some who have studied the source material at our disposal and have reached the conclusion that James Major never said anything. His brother John, in the beautiful Gospel that he wrote, doesn't mention James at all. And in all of Matthew, Mark and Luke we have only two sentences that might be attributed to James, though in both cases the words are said to have come from James and John together. In both cases it would have been better for the reputation of both men if they had not spoken at all. Let me tell you why.

Late one day Jesus and His disciples came to a village in Samaria, seeking lodging for the night. The Samaritans hated Jews, and the little company was rudely turned aside. "We don't want any Jews here. Get out!" As they left the village in the gathering twilight, a fierce and terrible indignation kindled in the hearts of James and John. It was felt by the others, too, but the two brothers put it into words: "Lord, shall we send fire from heaven, and consume them?" Ever afterward, Jesus called them "Sons of Thunder." He knew they loved Him, and hated His enemies. Still He reproved them. "You don't know what you're saying. I have come not to destroy men's lives, but to save them!"

It is something for us to remember. God wants us to be angry, angry with a righteous anger, against sin. He wants us to hate sin with a holy hatred. But He wants us to love the sinner, even as He loved sinners, and gave His only Son that sinners might be saved. There is too much bad feeling today, even within the Christian church. We don't like what people do or say and we begin to hate them for it. Or we become filled with indignation against a sinful world, the wickedness of some of our fellow-citizens, their dishonesty, their hypocrisy, their immorality, their utter indifference to the things of God and their very evident contempt for all of God's people, and soon we find ourselves saying, "Oh, what's the use? Let them burn. If they don't want to go to heaven, let them go to . . . well, let them go. Let them be forever condemned before the judgment throne of God! They're asking for it!" Or a minister will say to himself, "I've done what I could. I've tried. I've prepared messages to win them for Christ and save them from themselves and their own damnation. They don't come. They won't listen. They're not interested. They don't care!" I have heard disheartened, discouraged, broken-spirited pastors, in moments of near despair, confess, "There are times when I would rather dig ditches than keep on trying to lift a congregation to the throne of God or to save the unsaved. When I put my spade into the ground, it will accomplish something. When I dig a hole, it will stay dug." So we begin to share in the sin of James Major and His temperamental brother John. "Lord, send fire from heaven and let them be consumed!" And the Lord answers, "You don't know what you are saying. We are here to save our fellow-men, not to destroy them." And He means to tell us:

"We can't ever give up. Nor are we to judge our fellow-man. God will take care of that."

One day James and John, with their mother, Salome, said something else to Jesus for which He could only reprove them. "Let us sit at your right hand and your left hand," they said, "when you enter into your glory." They wanted places of prominence in the Kingdom of Heaven. They wanted to be the first among the Twelve in the realms of glory. And again Jesus said, "You don't know what you're asking. Can you drink the cup that I am going to drink and be baptized with the baptism that I am baptized with?"—in other words, "Can you suffer, as I am going to suffer? You who want so much of My glory, are you willing to share My Cross?" Glibly they answered, "We can! We are able." And Jesus answered, in effect, "Believe Me, you *will*." There were days, later on, when they remembered that. And then they heard Him say, "Whoever would be great among you must be your servant, and whoever would be first among you must be slave of all. For the Son of man also came not to be served but to serve, and to give His life as a ransom for many." This, too they remembered, and often, thinking of it in the years to come, they hung their heads in shame. Still there is striving for position within the Christian church; there are petty quarrels and jealous arguments, there is pride and selfishness and vanity in the hearts of His disciples. They have kept more people out of the church and they have driven more people away from the church than many of our more spectacular sins. People expect the Church, and they have every right to expect it, to be a fellowship of Christian love.

Before we think too poorly of James, let's remember that James was, in spite of everything we have said, a disciple particularly honored and respected and beloved of the Lord. He belonged to the Inner Circle within the Twelve, to the chosen three whose names again and again are linked together, to the privileged three whom Jesus often took with Him when the others were left behind: Peter, James and John—James was one of that blessed group. With the other eleven he watched and lived and breathed the whole wonderful ministry of the Son of God. With the other two he saw things the others didn't see. He was in the bedroom, the death chamber of the daughter of Jairus, who was ruler of the synagog. He saw Jesus take the cold, pale fingers of the little girl within His own strong, warm hand, and heard Him say, with a voice that even the dead must obey, "Child, I say to you, arise!" In the heart of James there was born in that moment the sure conviction, "This is the Prince of Life!" In that moment he knew and he could believe that for all those who are in Christ it is not death to die at all. "If anyone keeps My Word," Jesus had said, "he will never see death." Now James could see how that could be so.

There was another day when the chosen three had followed Jesus to the mountaintop, snow-capped Hermon, it was, where Jesus was transfigured before them, a glorious radiance playing about His form, and to the eyes of James there came a glimpse of heaven. That night James heard the voice of God, beheld for a dazzling moment the eternal glory of His Son, and swore to himself that never, never would he fail this Master who had shown Himself King of kings and Lord of all.

It was night again when Jesus led them to Gethsemane and they saw Him drink the bitter cup of torment, saw Him baptized with the baptism of tears and blood, saw Him being led as a lamb to the slaughter, destined, in less than twelve hours, to die for the sins of the world. It happened the following day, while James, with a breaking heart, saw them nail Him to a cross. He didn't know then that he would be the first, the first of the Twelve, to follow, and lay down *his* life for the Christian cause. Had he known, standing there beneath the cross, it would have made him glad. It would have been a comfort to him, in that dark hour, to know that he would share one day in the sufferings of Christ.

Share in them he did, seventeen years after his first meeting with the Master. By that time James Major, the silent disciple, had become a leader in the Church. When the storm breaks, lightning strikes the tallest trees and chimneys, things that stand out above the rest. When the storm of persecution broke upon the church at Jerusalem, and King Herod Agrippa was looking for someone of whom he could make a terrifying example, James was chosen for destruction and even Peter was placed second on the list. It was James who first drank of the bitter cup and was baptized with the baptism of blood. "I am able," he had said. "I can do it." He had *meant* that. When the time came, he went bravely to his death.

In his life very much like you and me, capable as you and I are even of cruelty and selfishness, in his fellowship with Jesus he rose to the heights, and in his death he is an example to us all. How many of us today are so full of our religion and so full of our love for Christ that we would be willing to die for Him? Yes, I said *die*. We, too, when we were confirmed, vowed ourselves willing to suffer all things, even death itself, rather than fall away from Him. And we took it all very lightly, because we were pretty sure that no one in this day and age and in this beloved land of ours would ever want to kill us because we are Christians. We were confident that the sword of Herod would never come near us. But the enemies of our Lord have other weapons, just as deadly, which are not made of steel. The world has a way of fighting religion, and fighting the church, by sneering at it, and making us ashamed to have a part in it. Suddenly we become unwilling to show our colors, embarrassed to be known as believing, practicing disciples of Christ. We are carried away by what someone has called "the easy-going paganism of modern life, which eats out the moral fiber and makes a man like a spiritual jellyfish." Or, as someone else has said, again and again we find ourselves unwilling "to stand up and be counted on the side which we know to be right, simply because there are so many thoughtless, empty-headed people on the other side," whose most effective weapon against us is their laughter or their scorn.

James Major, the silent disciple, quietly went to his death before he would renounce that Savior whose sacrifice of His own life's blood had opened for him the gates of the Kingdom of Heaven, whose death upon the cross had purchased for him all the joy and all the wonder of eternal life.

We who are like James in so many ways, especially in his sins . . . do we share his courage? Will we be faithful—to the end?

The serpent issuing from a cup indicates the attempt to kill John with poisoned wine.

John

I, John, your brother, who share with you in Jesus the tribulation and the kingdom and the patient endurance, was on the island called Patmos on account of the word of God and the testimony of Jesus.

REVELATION 1:9

JOHN

A man after the Lord's own heart.

JOHN would probably have agreed, if someone
had told him so to his face, that he was a small
man, a man of little importance, for the disciples
of Jesus were humble men. Lewis Mumford has
called them "the little men who guarded Jesus' memory." They were little men, he says, who took Jesus,
drained off the precious life blood of His spirit, mum-
mified His body, and over His remains proceeded to
erect the Christian Church. John wouldn't agree to
that. He would reject that assertion with every fiber
of his being!

We are becoming much better acquainted than we
have ever been before with these "little men" known
as the Twelve. We are bound to come, at the same
time, to a much better acquaintance with the Master
whom they served and followed. We are beginning
to see that they were not little men at all. They became, by the grace and power of God the Father, by
their intimate association with God the Son, and by
the wonderful inspiration of God the Holy Spirit, the

greatest and most influential men, aside from the Son of God Himself, ever to walk this earth.

John was one of the greatest of them all. In almost every language of the world his name is better known than any other. More children have been named for John than for any other saint or sinner in the whole history of the human race. It is a name happily shared by dozens of men and boys in any gathering today, all of them named for the John who walked with Jesus. John means "Jehovah has been gracious."

For some strange reason, John has been pictured in art and legend as a gentle, tender, soft-spoken, mild-mannered young man. He has been made almost effeminate, with a beardless, almost girlish face. Even Leonardo da Vinci has failed, I think, with John, whom he represents in his famed "Last Supper" as a full-faced effeminate youth, with something of a Mona Lisa smile on his face, his white hands meekly and languidly clasped together.

This is hardly the John whom we find in the Bible. This isn't the man whom we have seen as a boy, playing on the shores of the Sea of Galilee with his older brother James, where the boats were beached on the banks and the nets were hanging on their racks to dry. This isn't the lean and bronzed young fisherman of Bethsaida who sailed the deep and turbulent waters of that often rough and troubled sea. Shall we deny him firmness of flesh and hardness of muscle and manliness of voice because he was noted for a keenness of intellect and a depth of understanding of which the others were quite incapable? This intelligent young fellow who skilfully manned the fishing boats of his father Zebedee out there on the deep blue sea under a bright, hot sun, was he a tenderfoot, a softy, a man of putty, a spineless, lily-fingered, milk-and-water caricature of a man? Or is it likely that he became so, as some might infer, after leaving the ship and the sea and following in the footsteps of Jesus? Is that even remotely possible, when we know that the Twelve spent almost all of their time out-of-doors, living a hard and rugged life, on land and sea, in the company of that wandering Carpenter of Nazareth, Son of Man and Son of God, who Himself said that he had no place where He could lay His head? Remember, too, that it was John who, with his brother James, was called a son of thunder, for wanting to call down fire from heaven upon the Samaritan village that had cast them out when they had sought lodging for the night, cast them out because they were Jews. Listen to this, from one who has studied the life and character of the man: "Away with your effeminate pictures of an angelic John! He was a son of thunder, a devil-may-care youth who, whenever the storm was brewing, would have his boat out, who hurried to greet trouble, the kind of lad who in our day would have been in aviation or a member of the Foreign Legion!"

We have poker-playing, deep-drinking, Christ-cursing individuals today who sneer at the Christian religion as a pastime for women, children, and effeminate men. Why, they couldn't hold a candle to the manliness of the men whom Jesus gathered about Him! What about Christ Himself? What about the religion that He gave to the world at the cost of His own life? Here was a leader of men, here was a high and holy cause, for which, in the days of John himself, thousands were willing to lay down their own lives. For the sake of this Christ, for the confession of His holy name, they permitted themselves to be crucified. They placed their heads on the chopping block. They were boiled in oil. They were sewed into the skins of wild beasts and exposed to the fangs of mad dogs. They were covered with pitch and resin, nailed to pine posts and set afire as living torches in the imperial parks. They stood, silent and helpless, in the Roman arena, while shouting mobs were screaming for the release of hungry lions who would tear them to bits.

It wasn't really necessary. They could have escaped. Burn a little incense in the emperor's honor. Make believe that you never knew this Christ. That's all.—It was too much. They preferred to die. They would not deny Him. How could they deny Him, how could they refuse to die for Him who had died for them?

Their martyrs' blood transfused with living power the whole Christian Church! How could anyone put down that kind of faith, or vanquish a Christ who had awakened such devotion in the hearts of men?

If the church is marching on crippled feet today, stumbling and faltering where it ought to be going "from victory unto victory," always a little in trouble, always short of funds and manpower, never quite doing what it ought to be doing and could be doing for Christ and the sinner's redemption, it's because you and I today haven't begun to measure up to the manliness, the courage, the faith and love and loyalty and deathless devotion of men like John and the others of that glorious company. It's because you and I and our fellow-disciples in this easy and comfortable age have never quite learned what it means to offer actual sacrifices of self and substance to our blessed and holy Redeemer. We think we are doing God a favor when we interrupt our worldly routine once in a great while and show up in church. Some of us are ashamed to admit to fellow-workers at the shop or the office that we are church-members. Or, by some perverted process of reasoning, we think it a denial of our manliness to be clean and pure in word and conduct, to keep ourselves unstained from the world.

John was much more than merely a man of temper, a son of thunder. By all indications the youngest of the Twelve, he seemed to understand, far better than the others, what Jesus was trying to do and say. Mentally and spiritually they had a great deal in common. They breathed the same intellectual atmosphere. They were kindred spirits, these two, and I have a feeling that often, when Jesus was disturbed by the lack of understanding that He found in the others, John was a comfort to Him. John would give Him a quiet look that said, "I know what you mean."

So John belonged, with Peter and James, in that blessed group which we have called the Inner Circle among the Twelve, the three who saw so much the others didn't see. John was a man after the Lord's own heart, a man who dared to call himself, in the Gospel that he wrote, "the disciple whom Jesus loved." He loved them all, of course, but there was something special between Jesus and John. It was love that had sent the Son of God from heaven, love for a world that was lost in sin. It was love that sent Him to the cross to die for our salvation. It was a response of love that Jesus found in the heart of John. Still we know him as the apostle of love. To this day his words fall on our thirsting souls like rain on parched ground, "We love, because He first loved us. . . . Beloved, if God so loved us, we also ought to love one another."

In the company of Jesus, with that understanding heart of his wide open to everything that Jesus said and did, the man of temper became a temperate man, living a long and useful life, long after Jesus had ascended on high, long after the others had gone to heaven's rich and full reward. There are those who say that John lived to be a hundred or more.

We remember him for many things. We remember how he stood beneath the Cross, the mother of Jesus at his side. These two, more than all the others, so close to Him in so many ways, were closest to Jesus in His last agony, in the hour of His approaching death. The others were afraid, mentally and physically almost paralyzed with fear. But the woman whom He loved above all others, for she was His mother, and the man whom He loved because he was His most understanding disciple, stood close enough to the Cross even to hear Him speak. To them the noise and tumult of the mob were like distant thunder. Their breaking hearts were tuned to the breaking heart of Jesus. And this is what they heard Him say, while His ebbing life's blood was dripping into the ground at their feet, "John, take care of Mother when I'm gone. Mother, look upon him as your son."

They give citations and awards today for good or courageous behavior, for special service to communities and men. They honor great men with testimonial dinners. Never, never in human history, have greater honors been bestowed on anyone. To John, the dying Christ gave a special commission, a unique responsibility. The dying Redeemer laid upon His loving disciple a special burden of love. He was the man for it. Jesus knew that John would never disappoint Him, would never let Him down. Where was Peter in that moment? Where were the rest? We really don't know. We know that John was there, there to comfort and to bless, there to take from His Lord and Savior a special burden of love.

So often, when the Lord has need of us, when the King is looking for us, when the Redeemer of the world has work for us, when the cause of His Church and Kingdom puts demands upon us, we're just not there. We are conveniently busy doing something else, or we're not really close enough to Christ even to hear Him asking for us.

I know one way in which we can get closer to Him, closer to Him than we have been perhaps for a very long time. You go to church on Sundays. Thank God for that, for He has promised His living presence to those who gather together in His Name. He invites you to come even closer to Him in the blessed sacrament of Holy Communion. He wants to see you at the foot of the Cross. He wants to remind you of the sufferings and the death that purchased your salvation. He wants to give you the bread and wine of His holy Supper, and with it, His Body and Blood, His very self. How long has it been since you have received the blessing of Holy Communion?

There is still another way. This week, perhaps with His picture beside your Bible, read the inspired Scriptures that have come to us from the stylus of John. There is His Gospel, you know, his story of the life of Jesus, a very special one, quite different from the other three. Read his three letters, read them in a translation that you can really understand. Read his last book, the remarkable prophecy on which the Bible closes its pages, the Revelation of St. John the Divine, written from exile on the island of Patmos. Yon won't understand it all. Yet you will find in it passages of such grandeur, such comfort and hope, that you will cling to them till the end of your days.

John ended *his* days in Ephesus. Long after he could no longer preach a full sermon and had to be carried to his pulpit in a litter, he had just one message, tradition tells us, to satisfy the hunger of his people and to still their thirst, to calm their restless spirits. "Little children," he would say to them, "Love one another." Then he would say it again, "Little children, love one another."

He knew, as Jesus had known it, that there really is nothing more. "Little children, love one another!"

Philip's emblem contains the basket because of his reply to Jesus (John 6:7) when He fed the multitude.

Philip

The next day Jesus decided to go to Galilee. And he found Philip and said to him, "Follow me." Now Philip was from Bethsaida, the city of Andrew and Peter.

JOHN 1:43, 44

PHILIP

*His was the practical,
matter-of-fact approach.*

IT IS John who tells us everything that we know
about Philip. In the other three Gospels he is just
a name, one of the Twelve. In the Gospel of John
he becomes an individual, a personality, not nearly
as colorful as some of the others, but a personality
nevertheless. A Hebrew with a Greek name, he came
from Bethsaida on the Sea of Galilee, but he might
just as well have come from Missouri, for he was the
sort of man who had to be shown. This was no son
of thunder, like James or John. He was far too steady,
far too prone to keep himself within the limits of
careful calculation and common sense, like Peter to
rush in where angels feared to tread, making wild
promises and rash declarations, or dreaming great
dreams. He was the matter-of-fact disciple, for whom
we can have neither a great contempt nor an over-
abundant admiration. We end up liking him perhaps
because he was like so many of us today. He was
Mr. Average Christian, the one who comes to the
meetings and says, "Let's not be too hasty about this.

32

Let's give this thing a lot of thought before we take the plunge!"

Do you remember when Andrew followed Jesus, spent the rest of the day with him and then, perhaps late at night, ran home to his brother Peter, and brought him to Christ? It was on the very next day that Jesus found Philip and said to him, "Follow me." In such simple words the Gospel tells that wonderful story. This was one time that Philip did not hesitate. Philip had only to hear the voice of Jesus and look into His eyes to know that somehow his own life would never be the same again. In a moment Philip had gathered his belongings, put them into a kind of pilgrim's pack, slung it over his shoulder, and, with shining eyes, was walking at the side of Jesus, embarked on life's greatest adventure.

The next step, too, was inevitable. Even as Andrew felt compelled to share his joy with Peter, Philip, too, had someone with whom he *had* to share this wonderful experience, his friend, Nathanael-Bartholomew. "We have discovered him," Philip cried, "of whom Moses and the prophets wrote, Jesus of Nazareth, the son of Joseph." Nathanael laughed, for he had heard the word Nazareth. "Can anything good," he said, "come out of Nazareth?"

Philip was sick at heart. He had come with such a wonderful faith, such a boundless enthusiasm, only to be met with scorn and ridicule! How could he begin to convince this laughing friend of his that he,

Philip, had found the Messiah? Then the words came to him, the answer of a practical matter-of-fact man. "Come and see!" Forget about Nazareth. Come and see for yourself, and be convinced.

It is just here that we see Philip in the best light of all, as the new convert, the newly won disciple, eager to win someone else, eager to bring a friend to his new-found Savior. Actually, Philip didn't find Jesus at all. It was Jesus who found Philip. The Bible is very plain about that. Isn't that true of us, too? We don't find Jesus. He finds us. And when that happens to us, as it happened to Philip, when it *really* happens to us, when we know that the mercy of God has brought us to the Light of Life and the Wellspring of Salvation, when we know that by faith through grace we have come into fellowship with the Friend of Sinners and the Redeemer of Souls, we, too, want to share that experience with others. We become missionaries. We start to do mission work. We begin to talk church and religion to our friends.

Sometimes we find that this is a very unpopular subject, even with some of the people whom we have considered very good friends. They turn out to be most unappreciative of our interest in their spiritual welfare. They may even laugh at us, and that's what hurts most of all. "Good heavens! Look who's got religion! Don't tell me that you've found a church you like!" And they may tell you this: "I know all about churches. I don't want to have anything to do with them. The religion I have is in my heart. I don't need buildings and bells and books and pastors and pulpits. I don't care for the company of people who on Sundays spout a lot of pious prayers and sing a lot of dreary hymns and the rest of the week are no different from any of us!"

You feel exactly as Philip did when Nathanael said, "Can anything good come out of Nazareth?" For a moment the eager missionary finds himself tongue-tied. The devoted church-member, a new convert, perhaps, who has just been instructed and confirmed as an adult and is so happy about his new-found faith that he wants to share it with everyone, becomes hopelessly tangled up when confronted by the unbelief, the deepseated opposition against the church (which is in itself a kind of bigotry), or the laughing ridicule of some contemptuous friend. Then it's time to bring the reply of Philip. "Come and see. I may not be able to answer all your questions; I may not be able to talk down all your objections; I have no answer for your laughter; but I want you to come and see for yourself. Come with me to church. Come with me next Sunday morning and share one hour of worship with me. Come with me to the Pastor's Class. Give it a trial, for the good of your own soul." This is the practical, matter-of-fact approach. It wins people who couldn't be won by all the pious talk in the world. Ask them to "come and see." Tell them, "I'll call for you Sunday morning."

The practical, matter-of-fact approach has its limitations, too. I mean the over-cautious, too calculating approach toward church work. There was that day on the lake front, the day the crowd had grown larger and larger, till there were more than five thousand people there, listening to the words of Jesus. Suddenly it became apparent that these people could become a problem, too, for they were hungry, and they had nothing to eat. The practical solution was to send them away. It would have been quite like Philip for him to be thinking, "Why doesn't the Master get rid of them? Why doesn't He send them home?" It was Philip, the Gospel says, to whom Jesus turned and said, "How are we to buy bread, that these people may eat." It was said "to test him," we are told, for Jesus knew very well what He would do. It was a test that Philip failed. "Why," he stammered, "two hundred denarii would not buy enough bread for each of them to get a little." And he thought to himself, "Nor do we have the money. What's He thinking about, anyway?" Jesus turned from the practical disciple and his perfectly true and practical and common sense answer, to Andrew, who was standing there with a little boy at his side, a boy with a lunch basket that contained five barley loaves and two fishes. You know what happened. Jesus fed the whole crowd with that little boy's lunch. Philip was shamed to the depths of his soul. "I might have known! Why didn't I say to Him, 'Lord, this is a problem, as far as we are concerned, but it's no problem to you.' Why didn't I have that kind of faith!"

So often, in the work of the church, the completely

practical approach is one that only keeps us from doing what we *could* be doing and what we *must* do if the Kingdom of God and of His Christ is to prevail in the world of men. We dwell on our own weakness. We coldly calculate how little we are, how little we have, and how little we are willing to give and do, and we decide we'd better not try it at all. Let someone propose the opening of a new mission station in foreign fields, let someone dare to protest a really challenging budget to a Christian congregation which for a dozen years has been sitting on its hands and its purses, let someone dare to suggest the building of a great new church, in keeping with the glory of God and the magnificence of His Gospel, and immediately a dozen men like Philip will arise to say, "Why, you people are visionaries, you are impractical dreamers. It can't be done."

"Where there is no vision," the Bible says, "the people perish." The work of the Kingdom of God calls for faith and courage, initiative, determination, imagination! It demands, above all and first of all, an unfaltering belief in the sustaining, strengthening, helping grace and power of the God of miracles! It needs a sustained and continuing trust and confidence in the fact, so often forgotten and yet demonstrated again and again, that God's people, that Christ's redeemed, the members of His holy Church, given a great work to do, will do it, given a great challenge to meet, will meet it, and all because they know that they are not alone—they are fellow-workers with the living God and the living Christ in the redemption of the world. Philip looked at the crowd, at the problem, and forgot all about the power of Christ. Let's not make that same mistake when we plan our life, when we set out to do the work of God, when we build the walls of His Zion. Without Him— nothing! With Him and through Him—anything!

When we spoke of Andrew, we spoke, too, of the Greeks, the "aliens," the "outsiders" who came to Philip, possibly because he had a Greek name, and said, "We wish to see Jesus." Philip wasn't quite sure it was a good idea to let foreigners have access to the Master. He had to think this over first, or, better still, get someone else's opinion, have a talk with Andrew. In the meantime, the Greeks might have left, but that didn't bother Philip. "After all, we've got to be careful. We must not be too hasty." If they had left, it would have solved Philip's problem. There are some people who can be agonizingly slow in the face of great opportunities, and Philip, apparently, was one of them. He should have welcomed these people with open arms. He should have rushed to bring them to Jesus.

I remember, years ago, hearing about a little church congregation that never got anywhere. The members of the church had built their little place of worship and apparently wanted to keep it all to themselves. Visitors at the services received not a friendly welcome, but cold and repelling glances, as though the members meant to say, "What are you

doing here? This is *our* church! We're the ones who
went through the agony of the building program.
Why should we share all this with you?" I know it
has happened in larger churches, too, for some
strange reason known only to the devil and to God.
I hope it never happens here. I don't think Philip
was quite that bad. I'm sure that Philip, when Andrew revealed his own enthusiasm, was just as happy
about bringing the Greeks to Jesus as the Savior was
to receive them.

One final scene. Three years have passed, three
years of discipleship. They are in the Upper Room.
It is the night of one disciple's coming betrayal, the
night of the Master's approaching death. There is
nothing now but the Divine Plan to keep the breaking heart of Jesus from robbing the Cross of its
intended victim. Jesus is sorrowful, He tells them,
to the very point of death. "Having loved His own
who were in the world," John tells us later, "He loved
them to the end." And now He tells them that the
end is very near. They listen, wonderingly, fearfully,
and the tears run down their cheeks. He has just
washed their feet. Tenderly, lovingly, as though it
were a privilege, a high and holy task, the Master
has washed His disciples' feet. He has taught them
that most precious and priceless virtue, so little
known, so seldom practiced, the virtue of humility.
He has given them, there in the Upper Room, as an
everlasting remembrance, as a perpetual reminder to
all of His people for all time, the holy sacrament of

His Body and Blood. And then He speaks to them of the Father, the Father of whom He has so often spoken before, the Father to whom He is returning through the waiting portal of death, and of the many rooms in the Father's house, waiting, waiting for those who will follow in their Savior's footsteps. Suddenly Thomas interrupts with a question, and when it is answered, Philip, too, has something to say. "Lord," he says, "show us the Father, and we shall be satisfied." He wanted proof. His practical mind demanded a visible demonstration. And Jesus had it ready for him. Philip should have known it long ago. "Have I been with you so long, and yet you do not know me, Philip? He who has seen me, has seen the Father."

How often, in the dark house of sorrow, in the hospital's corridors of pain, in the wreckage of your life, have you said it: "O God, where are you? Lord, show me the Father!"

The answer is still the same. We who have seen Christ, have seen the Father. We who have stood at the foot of the Cross have seen the Father's redeeming mercy and forgiving love. We who believe in the Crucified and Risen and Ascended Christ know that all things work together for good to them that love God. And then we are satisfied.

The answer is still the same. But there are questions, too, terribly important questions: *Do* we see Him? *Do* we listen to Him? *Do* we believe?"

The three purses refer to Matthew's original occupation as a tax collector.

Matthew

As Jesus passed on from there, he saw a man called Matthew sitting at the tax office; and he said to him, "Follow me." And he rose and followed him.

MATTHEW 9:9

MATTHEW

*A most unlikely candidate
for discipleship.*

JAMES and John, Andrew and Peter were partners in the fishing business . . . James and John, Zebedee & Sons Company; Andrew and Peter, the Johnson Brothers. Theirs was a rugged business, a business for keen eyes, hard muscles, calloused hands, and a love of the sea. It meant knowing how to sail a boat through tumbling breakers, where to drop your nets and when to haul them in and how to gauge the weather. This was a man's business, whether there was money in it or not, a business for the kind of man who is willing to fight with the very elements in order to gain his livelihood. Such men, such men among men, Jesus chose for His disciples. Such men became the companions of the Carpenter of Nazareth who was also the Son of God.

He chose others, too. He chose a man like Matthew, who represented a kind of life much more like our own. Matthew, too, was a businessman, engaged in a kind of business with which many of us are familiar today. His was a business that dealt in cash

42

and accounting, that concerned itself with the things that Luther called "money and goods."

To be really specific about it, Matthew's business was collecting taxes. He collected taxes on the goods you brought into or took out of the country on the great trunk road from Damascus and the Far East to the Mediterranean Sea. You knew him, if you lived in Galilee; and if you were a Jew you despised him, for he collected taxes from you for the hated Roman invader. His customs office was in Capernaum, which happened to be Roman headquarters in Galilee. How well the banners of Rome were known and feared and hated in Capernaum, and the tread of marching soldiers from the Roman garrison! But it was good business, running the customs office, serving the department of internal revenue. "They hate you for it," Matthew and his fellow tax collectors would say to themselves and each other, "but there certainly is money in it!"

Everyone knew it was more than a little crooked. Men without conscience, men without scruples, had turned it into a colossal graft. Apparently they could collect what they wanted and keep as much as they liked. It was that easy. The Roman officials asked no questions as long as the money kept rolling in.

I often wonder what kind of a businessman Matthew was. He *was* a tax collector, and as such he shared in the general hatred toward his profession. He could have been an honest one. There were

honest businessmen in those days, just as there are
honest businessmen today. But it isn't very likely
that Matthew's skirts were completely clean. It was
simply taken for granted, in the days of Matthew,
that a Hebrew who would serve an alien government
in extracting tribute from his own people belonged
to the scum of the earth. He might get rich at it and
live in the best house in town, eat the best of food
and wear the finest clothing, but he was still the
scum of the earth.

To such a man Jesus came, while he was sitting at
his desk in the customs office, and said, "Follow me."
So Jesus gained another disciple. "He rose," the Bible
says, "and followed Him." It is that part of our Bible
which was written by Matthew himself. It is a kind
of confession on his part, this mention of his despised
profession; the other evangelists charitably forget to
mention it. It is a special kind of witness to us. "Such
and such a man I was," Matthew is telling us, "when
Jesus came and called me to Himself. In the opinion
of my countrymen I couldn't have been more con-
temptible. The business in which I was engaged
could not have been more suspect. There wasn't a
more unlikely candidate for discipleship in the whole
town. But He came and chose me."

You remember how Andrew, having found Jesus,
went and got Peter. You remember how Philip spoke
to Nathanael. Matthew tried it on a much larger
scale, by taking Jesus into his own home for a great
dinner party to which he invited all of his old friends.

In the Phillips translation the people who were invited are called "tax collectors and other disreputable people." If he were to explain it to us, Matthew would probably say, "I had three things in mind. I meant it to be a kind of celebration. I was so happy about having entered a whole new way of life. It was to be a kind of farewell, too, a formal announcement to my friends that I was no longer in business, certainly not in the mean and crooked business of sinking the talons of the Roman eagle into the tender flesh of my own countrymen. Most of all, though, it was a kind of desperate attempt to get the others to come along with me. Wistfully, and foolishly, I suppose, I hoped that my former friends, meeting Jesus at the dinner table, sitting down with Him later for a long talk, might become His disciples, too. Maybe, in those early days of my discipleship, I hoped to revolutionize the whole crooked tax collecting business overnight! Something I did accomplish, I know. They came, those friends of mine, utterly astonished at the step I had taken; they came ready to call me a complete fool. But they were eating my food and drinking my wine. They were polite enough, while partaking of my hospitality, not to laugh out loud or scold me too severely. They left, I know, with a new respect for the Master. They left knowing that everything He told them was true. They left and they did not follow Him, only because they were unwilling to pay the price."

Matthew *was* willing. Already in the customs office

the call of Christ was followed by an immediate decision. That very day, that very hour, perhaps that very moment, Matthew rose and followed Jesus. Was this an out-and-out miracle, a sudden surrender to impulse, an immediate submission to the power of a strangely compelling personality? Certainly it could have been, for Jesus had chosen Matthew as one of His own. I prefer to believe that it was more than a blind obedience to an irresistible compulsion. I prefer to think that Matthew knew a great deal about this prophet of Nazareth, who, like the Romans, had established headquarters in Capernaum. He was the talk of the town, as He was the sensation of the entire nation. Never had anyone spoken as Jesus spoke; never had anyone done what Jesus was doing. Day after day they came to Him, the soul-hungry thousands, to hang on His words and plead for His help. Help them He did, as no one had ever helped them before. The physically ill, the emotionally disturbed, the mentally deranged, the demon-possessed, He helped them all, and in His presence they found healing and peace. Words of love and mercy He spoke to them, the love and mercy of the Father and the love and mercy they were to have for each other. Certainly a rich and influential tax collector, known to all the people of that region and involved in all their affairs, would make it his business to find out what was going on.

It is more than likely therefore that Matthew had often seen and heard this Jesus, this Prophet of Nazareth. It is Matthew who, in his Gospel, gives us the fullest and most complete account of the Sermon on the Mount. Two chapters later he tells how he became the Lord's disciple. Isn't it likely then that Matthew, hearing and seeing Jesus again and again, gradually came under the Savior's spell? If he had heard nothing more than the Sermon on the Mount, it would surely have been enough. Isn't it possible that the hated tax collector, coming under the influence of Jesus, was learning to hate himself and everything that he was doing, and needed only the invitation of the Son of God to make a clear, clean break with everything that he had done before? I have a feeling that the break came long before he went home from the customs office for the last time. It came first in his heart! Maybe there were days when Matthew said to himself, "I wonder if He would accept me, if I came to Him." Then Jesus came to Matthew and made him His own.

Before that his name had been Levi, which means "joined." He had been joined all right, tied up with everything that was cruel and bad. Now he called himself Matthew, which means "gift of the Lord." Maybe it was his way of telling the world that this new life of his, this new life in Christ, was a "gift of the Lord." It always is, you know, whether it happens to a Levi who becomes Matthew or to you and me. Paul said it this way: "By grace you have been saved through faith; and this is not your own doing, it is the gift of God." Anyone who knows that, anyone who knows that this has happened to him, is going to spend the rest of his life saying in one way or another, as Paul said it, too, "Thanks be to God for His inexpressible gift!" Matthew, the business-man with the shady reputation, Paul, the self-right-eous Pharisee and persecutor of the infant Church, Luther, the troubled monk of Wittenberg, you and I, who know so well that even at our very best we are still sinners in the sight of God, don't we all belong to that strange and wonderful company who can only marvel at the divine mercy which has called us out of darkness into His marvellous light?

Matthew's business was so bad that he had to give up or he could not have become a disciple of Christ. It has happened again and again ever since. I hope your business isn't that bad. I hope it's the kind of business in which Christ Himself can become your business partner. I don't mean just giving God a tithe of your corporation income or a tenth of your profits. The world-famous Robert LeTourneau started with the tithe and became so successful that today he gives ninety per cent of his income to Christian churches and charities. It means even more than that, and this, too, LeTourneau did. It means building your business on Christian principles. It means taking Christ into the board room, to the conference table, into all your relationships with employees and customers. I like the title of a book I have about Robert LeTourneau. It is called "God Runs My Business." Does God run *your* business? Does God run *your* life?

You can choose to say "no" to that question. You can say that you're getting along very well all by yourself. Just remember this—if you think you can run your business without Him, if you think you can live without Him, you will have to die without Him, too. You will go to judgment without Him. You will have to spend eternity without Him. Read the story of the Last Judgment in the 25th chapter of Matthew's book. These are the words of Jesus: "Depart from me, you cursed, into the eternal fire prepared for the devil and his angels."

This, too, we know. That same Jesus, in utter defiance of public opinion, called the sinner Matthew to Himself. That same Jesus ate and drank with Matthew's disreputable friends. And when the self-righteous Pharisees threw up their hands in horror, He said to them, in effect, "But that's why I'm here, to call sinners to repentance." He came, He said, to seek and to save the lost. "If we confess our sins," John says, "He is faithful and just, and will forgive our sins, and cleanse us from all unrighteousness."

Matthew, like the rest, spent the remainder of his lifetime sharing that with all the world. Tradition says that his missionary journeys took him all the way to Ethiopia in Africa and, finally, to a martyr's death.

Matthew's legacy to all of us is the inspired Gospel

that bears his name. In it he gives convincing testimony to his own wonderful faith. "It's all there," he says. "It was all prophecied for us in the Old Testament. It was all fulfilled for us in Christ." It's still there, and it's there for you and me . . .

"Blessed tidings of salvation,
Peace on earth their proclamation,
Love from God to lost mankind."

Flaying knives in the emblem of Nathanael symbolize his martyrdom.

Nathanael-Bartholomew

Philip found Nathanael, and said to him, "We have found him of whom Moses in the law and also the prophets wrote, Jesus of Nazareth, the son of Joseph." Nathanael said to him, "Can anything good come out of Nazareth?" Jesus saw Nathanael coming to him, and said of him, "Behold, an Israelite indeed, in whom is no guile!"

JOHN 1:45-47

NATHANAEL-
BARTHOLOMEW

*He lived in the presence
of the living God.*

JOHN calls him Nathanael, the man whom we are to meet today; the other evangelists call him Bartholomew, which means "son of Tolmai." Nathanael is another name like John and Matthew. All of them convey the meaning: "gift of God." Nathanael-Bartholomew is little more than a name in the Gospel record. After we have been told how he became a disciple, we hear nothing about him at all except a casual reference on the part of John that he came from Cana in Galilee, a tiny village about five miles northeast of Nazareth. He is mentioned, of course, in the four lists of the disciples that we have from the inspired writers. Beyond that we have only conjecture and, here and there, a trace of his name in legend and tradition.

It is easy to take for granted, for example, that Nathanael, having come from Cana in Galilee, was present at the wedding-feast when Jesus performed the first of His miracles, turning water into wine. He would certainly have been known to the family of the bride. One obscure legend says that he was actually the groom; another story that someone has woven out of pure fancy pictures him as the disappointed suitor, the boy-friend who didn't quite make the grade.

The circumstances of his call make it plain that he knew nothing of Jesus of Nazareth until they were both adults, though apparently they had grown up within a few miles of each other. It is to me convincing evidence that all of the fanciful legends about the childhood of Jesus, the boyhood miracles, for example, among His playmates in Nazareth, of which tradition speaks so often and the Gospel not at all, are exactly that—fanciful legends and nothing more. The Bible speaks only of His amazing discussions with the doctors of theology in the temple at Jerusalem when He was twelve years old. Had Jesus, throughout His childhood and adolescence, revealed His divine nature among the people of Nazareth, Nathanael would have known all about it, and the people of Nazareth, who cast Him out in unbelief, would have behaved toward Him far differently than they did. It is just another testimony that we have to the truth of the Gospel record and a warning to us not to muddy the clear waters of our religion and its inspired source with the dubious and the doubtful, which is often a mere delusion. It is the great and priceless heritage of Protestantism to abide by the abiding Word.

Though his name is seldom mentioned and though

nothing he said or did is quoted, beyond the story of his first meeting with Jesus, Nathanael, we know, was one of our Lord's disciples, and, as such, he was permitted to enjoy a lifetime of priceless privilege for which many of us would be glad to offer our very lives. Nathanael did just that. Whether he was skinned alive, as pictured in ancient Christian art, or crucified in Armenia after preaching in India, as legend would have it, all of the ancient sources agree that he died a martyr's death. He died for the cause of Christ and His Kingdom.

All because he was one of the Lord's own. All because Jesus had called him to Himself and he had believed in Him and followed Him, had followed Him from the wedding table in Cana and the wine that had once been water to the communion table in the Upper Room and the wine which, Jesus told them, was His very blood. A three years' journey it was, weaving in and out of Judea and Galilee, the sun-drenched countryside, the tired villages, the squalid cities, the sick, the poor, the hungry, the proud and greedy people forming the warp and the woof for a tapestry that will hang in the halls of history and linger in the memory of man till time becomes eternity. Three years in the story of the human race, three out of all the thousands of years in which man has lived upon this planet; three years more momentous, more meaningful than all the others put together, they were Nathanael's, to spend with Jesus, Son of Man and Son of God, while Jesus went about

His God-given business of saving the world from its sins. He saw it all, and he listened, and each day he came to know more fully that he was sharing in the most fantastic experiences ever granted to mortal man. Miracle upon miracle, blessing upon blessing, hope and comfort, peace and power, and the promise of a victorious, triumphant eternity, day after day they went out from the heart and spirit of the God-Become-Man into the hearts and spirits of men who were seeking to come to God.

Nathanael was utterly mystified. Like the others, he often wondered, and yet he knew, knew that he was living, walking, eating, sleeping in the presence of the living God.

Then night fell, "the night in which He was betrayed," the night in which He washed their feet, gave them of His Body and Blood, through bread and wine, to eat and drink, and spoke with tearful eyes and breaking heart of His approaching death. That night they saw Him captured, beaten, bound and brutally led away. The next morning He carried a Cross to Calvary and His disciples, watching from a safe distance, felt as if they themselves, bound to that Cross, were being dragged through the streets of Jerusalem to their own death. But it was He who died, He who had so often spoken of living forever. It was He who died and, that day, their faith died with Him. That Friday night, and all of Saturday, they felt that they would never believe in anything again. They were like dead men themselves. They were physically alive, perhaps, but they were spiritually dead.

Then Jesus rose, and the miracle of the resurrection, forcing itself upon them as an incomprehensible and yet inescapable, irresistible and incontrovertible fact, restored them, rivived them, gave them a renewal of life and power that carried them to the ends of the earth with the message of God's love in Christ for the marvellous and merciful redemption of sinful man.

Nathanael was witness to it all. His name is mentioned, for example, among those who were fishing so fruitlessly one night after the resurrection. They had labored until dawn, and had caught nothing. Then, in the semi-darkness, they saw a stranger on the beach, who told them to try the right side of the boat. They did, and suddenly there were so many fish they couldn't haul in the net. In great excitement, John said to Peter, "It is the Lord!" At once Peter plunged into the sea and swam toward shore, and the others rowed, dragging the net full of fish. That morning they breakfasted with the risen Jesus; that morning He said to them, and especially to Peter, "Feed my sheep, and my lambs." That morning Peter knew that he had been restored to discipleship and Nathanael, listening, knew that love like this was love that had to be shared with all the world.

It had all begun three years before. In those days Nathanael was certainly no man of the sea, like Peter and Andrew, James and John; more likely, he was a vine-dresser or a keeper of vineyards, lover of plants and trees. Some say he was the quiet, contemplative type, the kind of man who would enjoy sitting under the broad, cool leaves of the family fig tree, deep in prayer, devout in his meditation on the promised coming of the Kingdom of God. We don't really know. But this is what happened.

One day his friend Philip came to him, all excited. He could hardly wait to say what he had to say: "We have found Him of whom Moses and the prophets wrote, Jesus of Nazareth, the son of Joseph." How well Nathanael knew Nazareth—poor, pitiful, utterly unimportant Nazareth—too well, apparently, for it brought a derisive, cynical question to his lips. "Did you say Nazareth? Can anything good come out of Narazeth?" Philip said, "Come and see." Maybe it was pure curiosity, maybe it was for friendship's sake, but Nathanael went to see.

They were still some distance away when Nathanael, looking up the road toward the group of people to whom Philip was steering him, heard a man say, "Behold, an Israelite indeed, in whom is no guile!" In the Phillips translation it sounds like this, "Now here is a true man of Israel; there is no deceit in him!" Nathanael drew near, looked into the smiling eyes of Jesus, and knew at once that he had entered into the presence of Someone who knew him through and through, knew him and liked him and wanted him for His own. Nathanael had sounded cynical to Philip, even contemptuous, but his contempt had been all for Nazareth. As for his doubts, he had been perfectly honest and utterly sincere. After all, one who has spent years in the study of the Law and the reading of the Prophets, waiting and hoping and praying for the fulfillment of the promises, can hardly be expected to be profoundly impressed when a friend comes with a hasty and bland announcement that the Messiah has suddenly appeared, from some utterly ridiculous place not even mentioned in the Old Testament. Nazareth!! Bethlehem, perhaps, Bethlehem of Judea, that would be something else again, for so it was written. *That* a person might begin to believe.

His honest doubts, his sincere bewilderment, his open questions vanished in the presence of Christ and gave place to complete amazement: "How do you know me?"

Jesus answered, "Before Philip called you, when you were under the fig tree, I saw you." This was a miracle. This was the answer to a lifetime of prayer. Nathanael's whole spirit rushed out to meet the love that was pouring from the heart of Jesus. "Rabbi," he said, "Master, you are the Son of God! You are the King of Israel!" Jesus spoke again, to a man who in that moment had become His disciple. "Because I said to you, I saw you under the fig tree, do you believe? You shall see greater things than these." He was quiet for a moment, and then He went on, "Truly, truly, I say to you, you will see heaven opened, and the angels of God ascending and descending upon the Son of Man."

There are so many Nathanaels today, men without guile, without deceit, likable, lovable people, who are completely honest and perfectly sincere when they say to us, "I'm sorry, but I just don't believe." "I can't lie about this," they may tell us. "The simple truth of the matter is that I just don't believe." Sometimes they are frank enough to let us know that they feel about the church as Nathanael felt about Nazareth, and with a kind of bitter humor they may say to us, "Can anything good come out of the church?" You see, they've had a bad experience with the church, or with the church's pastors and people, or they've been brought up with all kinds of misunderstandings and misinformation about the church and religion. Nathanael knew only bad things about Nazareth. He apparently didn't know, or didn't care, or didn't bother to find out that Nazareth was the home of good people like Joseph, the carpenter, his wife Mary and her son Jesus. There are a lot of people who think and know only bad things about the church and when you talk religion to them they let you know that they are not interested. Actually they are. They must be. They are God's creation. They are God's children. Many of them will confess that they pray every day.

Do you know what they need? They need to see Jesus—not us poor examples, us pitiful specimens, us weak and sinful disciples who stand around Him, and sometimes stand between Him and those who ought to be finding Him—but Jesus. They need to see Jesus. You and I had better remember that, and remember that we must help them to see Jesus. It means that we must be as Christlike as we possibly can in our personal life. Above all, it means that you and I must say to them, as Philip said to Nathanael, "Come and see."

If they are people without guile, if they are honest and sincere, they will come. They will give Him a chance to show Himself to them. They will learn in time that He is Son of God and Savior of the world, King of kings and Lord of lords. And some day, for this is His own promise, they will see heaven opened, and the angels of God ascending and descending upon the Son of Man

Are you one of them—one of the Nathanaels of the present day? Come and see. For Jesus said, "All that the Father gives Me will come to Me; and him who comes to Me I will not cast out. For this is the will of My Father, that every one who sees the Son and believes in Him should have eternal life; and I will raise him up at the last day."

The sailing vessel represents the many missionary journeys ascribed to the apostle by church tradition.

Judas, 'not Iscariot'

Judas (not Iscariot) said to him, "Lord, how is it that you will manifest yourself to us, and not to the world?"

Jesus answered him, "If a man loves me, he will keep my word, and my father will love him, and we will come to him and make our home with him."

JOHN 14:22, 23

JUDAS, 'NOT ISCARIOT'

A name and a question.

WHAT'S in a name? Sometimes nothing at all. Sometimes a whole lot. It all depends. What's in a name like Judas? The shocked amazement, the horrified judgment, the pitiless contempt of the whole civilized world. Ever since a certain Judas of Kerioth, for a handful of silver coins, agreed to betray a certain Jesus of Nazareth into the hands of His enemies, the name Judas has aroused nothing but feelings of hatred, of bitter distaste. Even charitable minds who have tried to explain to themselves and to the world how this could possibly happen, have never succeeded in making a saint out of Judas Iscariot. The halo just doesn't fit. It keeps falling off.

Did you know that there were *two* disciples by the name of Judas? And did you notice how careful John is to tell us that the Judas of whom he is speaking to us today is "Judas 'not Iscariot' "? Is it because he wants to spare him the shame of identification with that other Judas who betrayed his Lord and Master? Judas, or Jude, was a popular name in those days. Today we know it only in the beautiful feminine form

62

of Judith. Nowadays there seems to be at least one little Judy in every block. But the name Judas has disappeared. Neither I, nor, I believe, any other minister of recent times has ever baptized a baby boy with the name of Judas. Peter, James, John—there are dozens of them everywhere. But Judas? You wouldn't think of calling your son Judas! There were two Judases among the Twelve, Judas Iscariot and Judas 'not Iscariot,' who was also called Lebbaeus or Thaddaeus, which means "from the heart," or "One beloved," and was a term of endearment.

We who seem to know so much about the hated Judas, what do we know about this Judas, the beloved? Beyond his name nothing at all, nothing except a question that John says he put to the Lord in the Upper Room. A name and a question, that's all. This is the full extent of the biographical material at our disposal—one sentence, a name, a question; and the answer of the Lord. But John wants us to be sure to remember that this is Judas "not Iscariot."

When I was quite young, a physician whom I respected and liked very much used to say to people who were taking themselves and their problems too seriously, "Don't worry about it. A hundred years from now no one will remember that you ever lived." That can be bad advice as well as good. It can lead us into all kinds of trouble. But the assertion, damaging as it is to an inflated ego, is true. How many people, a hundred years from now, will bother to remember that we ever lived? It has been said that more books have been written about Abraham Lincoln than about any other mortal who ever lived. It has also been said about Martin Luther. But these men are the exceptions to the general rule. No one is going to write biographies of you and me. Think of it! There is a disciple of the Lord Jesus Christ, one of the Twelve, of whom we know nothing but a name and a question. But this much we do know. He was Judas "not Iscariot." There's a lesson in that for you and me.

For a while they *will* remember us, the folks we leave behind when we fall asleep for the last time to be awakened, not by the jangle of tomorrow's alarm, not by the insistent buzz of that little electric monster, but by the trumpets of the living God at the dawn of eternity's day. Some of them will remember us for a while when we're gone. What will they remember? Will it be good? When they sum up the story of our life in a sentence or two, as people often do, where will they put us—with Judas Iscariot, or with Judas "not Iscariot"? What do people say about us now, when we are not around? You've heard them. Someone mentions a name, and immediately someone else says, "I remember him; he's the one who's always cursing; can't utter a sentence without being either filthy or profane!" Another name is mentioned and immediately you remember that he became the town drunkard and lost his family, his business, and ruined his whole life through addiction to drink. Another name brings to mind the worst gossip you have ever known, a woman who found an evil delight in malicious talk. Still another causes someone to say, "You mean that fellow who was always causing trouble in the church back home? I remember him. I'll never forget him." Thumbnail sketches, single-sentence biographies they are, and they are not pretty.

There are others, thank heaven, of whom we think with warm and grateful hearts, and with a little pang of sorrow if we know that they've gone beyond, people whom we fondly remember as the kindest, the most generous, the most cheerful, the most truly Christian, the most faithful, unselfish individuals that it has ever been our pleasure to know, the best mother, the most capable father, the most understanding teacher, the most admirable businessman, the most humane physician, the most sincere pastor, the most devoted churchworker in our acquaintance.

This much we had better keep in mind. The life that is given to us now, the hours that are yours and mine today, the days and the weeks that are passing for us this year, the discipleship with Jesus that we are living out right now, will decide for time and for eternity whether we will be remembered with Judas Iscariot or with Judas "not Iscariot." Yes, I said for time and for eternity. There are only two alternatives. We will spend eternity with the blessed or with the damned, with Christ or without Christ, depending on whether we have believed or have not believed, whether we have walked with God, by grace through faith, in "the light of the knowledge of the glory of God in the face of Jesus Christ" or have chosen not to walk with God, in the darkness of our unbelief.

Beyond the name of Judas "not Iscariot," we have only the question that he asked of Jesus in the Upper Room. It was the darkest night in the history of man, the night when God's own Son tried to explain to the men who had been following Him that He was about to die so that the hearts of men need never be wholly dark again. Perhaps it was darkest of all that night in the hearts of His loving and beloved disciples. They just didn't understand. They were terribly afraid. For the Master was talking of dying, in tones of a heartbroken determination more solemn than anything they had ever heard from Him before. Judas—Judas Iscariot—had been sent from the room, with these words of Jesus following him into the night, "What you are going to do, do quickly." The other Judas shuddered as he saw his namesake go. What did it mean? What was to come of all this?

Then he heard the Master say, "Where I am going you cannot come." He was going away, then. He was going to leave them. It was the announcement of His imminent death and the death, His disciples thought to themselves, of all their hopes and dreams. But Jesus was talking about something else now. "A new commandment I give to you," He was saying to them, "that you love one another; even as I have loved you, that you also love one another. By this all men will know that you are My disciples, if you have love for one another." But an aching loneliness wrapped itself around Judas, for he had heard the Master say, "Where I am going you cannot come."

But then there came comfort, too, blessed comfort and radiant hope, for the voice of Jesus went on, "Let not your hearts be troubled; believe in God, believe also in Me. In My Father's house are many rooms. . . . I go to prepare a place for you. . . . I will not leave you desolate; I will come to you. Yet a little while, and the world will see Me no more, but you will see Me; because I live, you will live also. In that day you will know that I am in My Father, and you in Me, and I in you. He who has My commandments and keeps them, he it is who loves Me; and he who loves Me will be loved by My Father, and I will love him and manifest Myself to him." They were wonderful, beautiful words, too wonderful, too beautiful for comprehension. What did it mean? It was Judas who asked. "Lord," he said, "how is it that you will manifest yourself to us, and not to the world?"

Jesus answered, "If a man loves Me, he will keep My word, and My Father will love him, and we will come to him, and make our home with him." It was exactly what Jesus had said before. No use trying to explain . . . no use trying to tell them just how it would all come about . . . just this: "Take comfort, Judas, and don't be afraid. Tomorrow you will see Me die. But you will not be left alone. I will come to you, and I will be with you, as long as you love Me and lovingly keep My word."

In all the history of this hurtling planet, in all the story of the human race, only one man could dare to talk like that, the God-Man, Jesus Christ. This was the answer of One who could look beyond Mount Calvary to Olivet, beyond the hill of His death by crucifixion to the mountain of His ascension, where, triumphantly and gloriously risen from the dead, He could say to His apostles, "All authority in heaven and on earth has been given to Me . . . lo, I am with you always, to the close of the age."

Perhaps not that very night in the Upper Room, but surely later on, Judas learned to know what Jesus meant, when, through all the fiery trials and crushing tribulations of his apostleship, he learned to feel the sustaining, strengthening, life-giving presence of Jesus wherever he labored, wherever he suffered, wherever he went . . . when, in the years that followed Pentecost, by faith and prayer, by Word and Sacrament, he knew that Jesus was ever at his side.

Isn't this just where our discipleship so often falls down today? We forget that Jesus has promised His unseen presence to those who love Him and keep His word. We come to church and we go through all the motions of worship, singing, praying, bringing our tithes and offerings—we listen to the Word of God, if we find it interesting and we're not too tired, and we do it all in a way that shows that we are not even half conscious of the presence of Him who said, "Where two or three are gathered in My name, there am I in the midst of them."

More important still, we live out our life in a way that shows we have half forgotten or we just don't believe that Jesus is living today, that He knows how things are with us from hour to hour and from day to day, that He knows us and what we are doing, what we are saying, reading, thinking, planning, that He knows and that He's interested. We have heard too much of the world's ridicule. We have tasted too deeply of the world's unbelief. We have tried to take the supernatural out of our religion and we have succeeded only in robbing ourselves of the presence of Christ. Wasn't that Christ's answer to the question of Judas? "If a man loves Me, he will keep My word, and My Father will love him, and we will come to him and make our home with him." So do Christ and the Father manifest themselves to us and not to the world. The Phillips translation says "make themselves real" to us.

In the loneliness of his imprisonment, forsaken by most of his friends, Paul could say, "But the Lord stood by me and gave me strength. . . . The Lord will rescue me from every evil and save me for His heavenly kingdom!"

Stephen, bruised and bloody, being stoned to death for his faith, looked up to what others saw as an empty sky and said, "Behold, I see the heavens opened, and the Son of man standing at the right hand of God."

What was it that Judas had asked? "Lord, how is it that you will manifest yourself (that you will 'make yourself real' to us), and not to the world?" This was the answer, the answer that has come to His disciples ever since, disciples who have loved Him and kept His word.

The Father and His beloved Son have promised to come and make their home with us. The eternal Christ is with us when we worship Him. He hears us when we pray. He walks at our side. "Yea, though I walk through the valley of the shadow of death, I will fear no evil, for Thou art with me." The Shepherd leads us, and the Father is waiting, there on the other side.

But we must love Him, and keep His word.

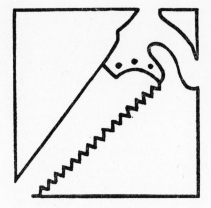

The emblem signifies the tradition that the head of James was sawed from his body during Christian persecutions.

James Minor

There were also women looking on from afar, among whom were Mary Magdalene, and Mary the mother of James the younger and of Joses, and Salome, who, when he was in Galilee, followed him, and ministered to him; and also many other women who came up with him to Jerusalem.

MARK 15:40

JAMES MINOR

*Among those who won
the world for Christ.*

THEY call him James "the younger" today, in the modern translations. In the Greek of the Gospel according to St. Mark the reading is James "the little." Some say it is to be taken literally, that this James must have been a little fellow, the kind of man who is nicknamed "Shorty" in our day. He has also been called James the Less, and James Minor, to distinguish him from that other James who was a brother of John, often called James Major. His father's name was Alphaeus, which was also the name of Matthew's father; yet nowhere are we told that James and Matthew were brothers. His mother's name was Mary; she was one of the Marys who went to the tomb on Easter morning. These are the facts at our disposal. We have discovered that we know very little about some of the disciples. About Judas "not Iscariot," for example, we know only his name and a question that he asked of our Lord. We know even less about James Minor. He has often and rightly been called "the unsung saint." We can think of him as "the forgotten follower."

In all likelihood there were *three* men by the name of James who were close to Jesus, James Major, James Minor, and, later on, the James who is called "the Lord's brother,"* and wrote the New Testament letter which bears his name, becoming a pillar of the church at Jerusalem under the name of James the Just. The identity of these men has often become confused in the art and tradition of the centuries. In our meditations on the Twelve we have chosen to remain with the established facts of Biblical history. It means that we know almost nothing at all about James Minor.

Does that trouble you? Does it disturb you to discover that the Bible doesn't answer all our questions, doesn't tell us everything that we would like to know? Some people, at this very point, have suffered spiritual shipwreck and have lost their faith. "There are too many unanswered questions, too many things I don't understand."

In reference to this very thing, I once heard the president of a well-known university say, "We must refer the questions of time to the answers of eternity." University presidents are presumably intelligent people. I have often pondered that statement, and it has been a great comfort to me. We *all* have unanswered questions. How often the Twelve were baffled, perplexed. Living with Jesus, enjoying the most intimate fellowship with the Son of God, every day they saw things and they heard things they just didn't under-

---

*Gal. 1:19; cf. Matt. 13:55 and Mark 6:3.

stand. And so they plied Him with questions. You've asked them, too—I know you have, because *I* have, the questions that say to God, "What's it all about? Why is it so hard to understand?" or that other question which dares to wonder even about the goodness and the mercy and the wisdom of the eternal God, the question that says, "Why? Why does God let this happen to me?" or "Why doesn't He answer my prayers?" which really means, "Why doesn't He do as I say?"

One of the most intelligent Christians who ever lived was an adult convert by the name of Paul, University of Tarsus, Class of Thirty-Something-Or-Other, a postgraduate student of the great philosopher, Gamaliel. Paul had lots of unanswered questions. There were many things he didn't understand. But Christ had come to him and he had come to Christ, and it made all the difference in the world. He was sure of his salvation. It was all that really mattered. "I know whom I have believed," he writes to Timothy, "and I am sure . . ." and to the Romans, "I am not ashamed of the gospel: it is the power of God for salvation to every one who has faith." Unanswered questions, perplexing problems? Of course. Paul was intelligent enough to know that he wasn't God! But he knew that some day his questions would be answered and he was willing to wait. It was Paul who said, "Now we see in a mirror, dimly, but then face to face. Now I know in part; then I shall understand fully, even as I have been fully understood."

Why this confidence? Why this beautiful, humble, childlike trust from so great a man?

He wasn't in the Upper Room on the night before Jesus died. But years later he spoke with those who were there, when he had come at last to share their faith. And they told him what Jesus had said. "He was about to make His journey to the Cross," they said. "He knew that on the following day we would be passing through the most soul-shattering experiences of our entire discipleship. And this is what He said to us, 'So you have sorrow now, but I will see you again and your heart will rejoice, and no one will take your joy from you. In that day you will ask me no questions.' That's what He said, *'In that day you will ask me no questions.'*"

I wonder if Paul ever said to the people about him, "You know, the older I get, the more content I am to wait. After all, it isn't going to be long any more. In a very short time I shall be with Christ, when all my questions will be answered." I'm sure there are many of us who feel that way. I have my unanswered questions. I may not know very much, for example, about James the Less, but I know enough about Jesus Christ to know that He is the Son of God and the Savior of the world and my own personal Redeemer. I believe that, with all my heart, and, believing it, I am perfectly willing to refer the unanswered questions of time to the divinely promised answers of eternity.

The fact that we have in the Bible disciples of

whom we know almost nothing at all can actually be very comforting to us. You and I are not likely to be remembered very long after we die. Does it mean that everything we do today is done in vain? Doesn't it point out to us that the discipleship with Christ that we are living out today is all-important? Was James a failure in everything he did simply because he went to his grave and was forgotten? Maybe it will be good for us to call to mind that some of the greatest benefactors of mankind are utterly unknown today.

Who was it, for example, in the dim forgotten past, who invented the wheel? Who was it that first discarded the rude and clumsy ox-drawn sledge and fashioned the first rough wheel? He was a pioneer of civilization, one of the greatest inventors that ever lived. Almost all the inventions of modern times depend in some measure on the wheel. Most of you came here on wheels and you came on time because a little box of wheels on your wrist or on the kitchen wall proclaimed the hour; the wheels of industry give you a livelihood; the wheels of agriculture provide you with foodstuffs; the wheels of commerce bring them to your table. The army rolls on wheels; even ships and airplanes are helpless without them. Take away the wheel and civilization goes back to the stone age and the life of the cave man. Who invented the wheel?

Who preserved the Bible for us? Who were the humble, faithful men, in the early centuries of the church's history, who sat in their cold and cheerless cells, hour after hour, day after day, and wrote and wrote and wrote, copying by hand, with painstaking care, the sacred words of the inspired Scripture, keeping alive, for unnumbered generations of sinners yet unborn, the gospel of the pardoning mercy of God in Jesus Christ, His Son? Who were they? What were their names?

How many of us know the names of those responsible for bringing the faith to America, the brave pioneers who brought the divine Word to the plains and forests of the New World, who braved every hardship, faced every danger, who were willing even to die, as many of them did, that the good news of the Gospel might find a new home and gain new converts in the land of the free? We glory today in the heritage which they have transmitted to us, the faith that is flourishing from shore to shore of this vast land. The church that they planted in the wildwood has become a mighty evangelical force, preaching the Gospel of the Kingdom to the ends of the earth. And we've forgotten their names.

We see a great church, a tower of strength in the community, the most wholesome force in the life of the people who live within its shadow. Who founded that church? We don't know. And before long we realize that it doesn't matter. It isn't the name that counts. It's the work that was done, the souls that were saved, the gospel that was preached . . . these are the things that matter.

We might well remember that, you and I who are engaged in what people call the thankless work of the church. We will probably never get very much credit for the work we do, the hours we put in, the midnight oil we burn for the cause, the sacrifices of time and toil and talent, the cost in nervous energy and cold, hard cash. We may give more than a tenth of our income to the Lord and devote more than a tithe of our time to His work and get little more than scorn and ridicule from some of our friends, and then we shall go to our graves to be forgotten. But sinners will have been saved from eternal perdition. God's work will have been done and will continue to be done, because, when we had the chance, when we lived our life, we made our contribution, we did our share, we helped along.

It really doesn't matter, you know, whether people will remember you and me. But it *does* matter that they learn to know our Lord and Savior Jesus Christ. "This is life eternal," Jesus said to His Father in prayer, "that they know Thee, the only true God, and Jesus Christ whom Thou hast sent."

Someone has written, "This is what will make good workmen of us all, to be impressed with the majesty of Jesus, the supremacy of the Kingdom of God, and the eternal worth-whileness of contributing our share to the advancement of that Kingdom."

We are not quite sure who James Minor was. We know very little of what he did. He was a disciple of Jesus. He was one of those who won the world for

Christ. Apparently he wasn't the kind of soldier who wins a lot of medals. If there are monuments and memorials in his name, I don't know where they are. But I know that this word of God is forever true: "Those who are wise shall shine like the brightness of the firmament; and those who turn many to righteousness, like the stars forever and ever!"

Simon is represented by a fish, for he was a fisher of men; by the book to indicate his Gospel preaching.

Simon Zelotes

Simon who was called the Zealot.

LUKE 6:15

SIMON ZELOTES

A political fanatic.

W E HAVE already become acquainted with two disciples by the name of James, one well-known, the other almost entirely unknown. We have discovered that there were two men among the Twelve called Judas, one notorious, the other almost forgotten. Did you know that there were two Simons? One of them you know. Everyone knows him. Even the man on the street who has never been inside a church knows, or thinks he knows, the Simon whom Jesus called Peter, the Rock. He has probably never heard of the Simon whom we are to meet today, and perhaps you haven't either.

The Bible introduces him to us four times, in the four lists that we have of the apostles, twice as Simon the Cananaean and twice as Simon the Zealot. Scholars are now pretty well agreed that the two words mean the same thing, "Cananaean" coming from the Hebrew and "Zealot" from the Greek. Phillips, in each of the four lists, uses just one word, and calls Simon "Simon the Patriot." Actually, it designates him as a member of a certain political party. In our day it would be Simon the Republican, or Simon the Democrat, or Simon the Communist.

Are you surprised at the use of the word Communist? We think of Communists today as members of a party which advocates the overthrow of our government. We have been taught to think of them as people to whom treachery, cruelty, violence and bloodshed are the accepted tools which they will use without hesitation to achieve their ends. Certainly this Simon, a disciple of Jesus, was no Communist! The Bible calls him a Zealot, a member of the Patriot Party. And this is where we come in for a real surprise. For the Zealots or Patriots had just one aim, one goal: to deliver Judea from the yoke of Roman bondage, to drive the Roman legions from the Jewish homeland, to tear the Roman banners from the flagstaffs of Jerusalem. Organized by a rabid revolutionary called Judas of Galilee about twenty years before the beginning of Christ's ministry, they became in time an "underground" movement so ruthless and violent in character that they did the cause of Jewish freedom far more harm than good. The murders they committed, the sabotage they perpetrated, resulted, finally, in the total destruction of Jerusalem by vengeful Roman authorities.

One of them was a disciple of Jesus, "Simon, who was called the Zealot," Simon the Patriot. There was a revolutionary, a political fanatic, among the Twelve.

How often the world has been set on fire by political fanatics! How often humanity has suffered the frightful consequences of flaming nationalism, when a few men in high places have decided that certain races are purer than other races and that certain nations are better than other nations, and deserve to rule the world! Again and again in the history of the world that fanatic philosophy has resulted in devastating human conflict. Class wars, race hatreds, strife between capital and labor, between Jew and Gentile, white and black, soldier and civilian, these things the Zealots give us, the ruthless fanatics.

How often the church, too, perhaps even more than the world, has suffered from fanaticism! It was blind fanaticism that changed Christianity from a persecuted into a persecuting church. It was a misguided zeal that gave rise to the power of the bishops of Rome and all the subsequent sins and abuses of the papacy. It was a blood-thirsty loyalty to the church that devised the tortures of the Spanish Inquisition and the heresy trials of the Middle Ages, when hundreds were broken on the rack or burned at the stake; that made an outcast of Martin Luther, with the excommunication of a pagan pope and the ban of the emperor hanging over his head; that refused to heed the pleas of Protestant reformers and gave rise to the bloody wars of religion that devastated Europe for so many years. It was fanaticism within the ranks of Protestantism that ruthlessly destroyed, over the vigorous protest of Martin Luther, priceless treasures of Roman Catholic art and architecture. It was fanaticism that caused the very men who came to America for freedom of worship and religion to instigate the heresy trials and the witch-hunts that darken and stain the pages of our country's early history. It is a misguided zeal of another kind, no matter how sincere and how well-meant, which is harming the church today, the emotional sensual, foaming, jumping, rolling, stomping, snake-handling, Hallelujah-shouting type of Christianity which can only bring down upon itself the derisive laughter or the pitying contempt of thinking men and women who need to be won for Christ and brought into His Kingdom. Deliver the world and the church from fanatics! How often, thinking they were helping, they have done irreparable harm to the cause of Christ!

What about that zealot among the Twelve? It is possible that he became a disciple because he hoped to use Jesus, because he saw in Christ and the amazing power of Christ all the potentialities for the revolution which he hoped would some day sweep the Romans out of Palestine. Somehow he sensed that this Jesus was a revolutionary, too. In the minds of many Hebrews the whole concept of Messiahship had left the realm of religion and gone into politics. Many of the people who followed Jesus wanted to make him their earthly king, a champion who would rid them once and forever of the Roman yoke. Maybe that's why Simon became a follower of Jesus.

Jesus *was* a revolutionary! He *had* come to establish a Kingdom!

Simon learned in time that it was a Kingdom "not of this world." Living with Jesus, in that wonderful fellowship that blessed companionship, he came to know that this was the Messiah all right, but that the Kingdom of Messiah was a spiritual kingdom to be established not by force but by the power of divine love working in the hearts of men. In time he came to believe what at first he had found so hard to understand, that this Jesus had come from another world, from God's world, that He was in very truth the Son of God Himself, sent by the heavenly Father to save the world from sin. He had hoped that Jesus would establish a throne in Jerusalem, even if it required the shedding of the blood of men. After all, isn't that the way kings are made and thrones are established and empires are built among men? Instead Simon learned that Jesus was destined, by the shedding of His *own* blood and the sacrifice of His *own* life, to redeem the souls of men from sin and from the eternal consequences of sin and make them kings and priests with Him forever, in the heavenly Jerusalem.

In short, Simon the Zealot became a man transformed, transformed by the power of the Savior's love. He was still a Patriot, but it was no longer the Kingdom of Judea for which he was willing to work and fight—it was the Kingdom of God and of His Christ. The struggle was no longer with Rome but with sin, and its object was no longer mere freedom from the yoke of human bondage, but the freedom

of the spirit which has found forgiveness in Christ
and eternal sonship with God the Father. It is said
of Simon that he became an ardent missionary and
apostle, preaching principally in Mesopotamia. Legend says that death came to him in Persia, where he
joined those martyrs of the faith who died in a manner particularly abhorrent to us and certainly terrible
to its victims. They sawed him in half.

Now let's bring it up to date. This is the story of
a man completely transformed by his encounter with
Christ. It happens today and, if you still need that
kind of transformation, it can happen to you. There
isn't anyone who can't be transformed by the mercy
of God into a believing, practicing Christian, a disciple of Christ who has come to know that life's
highest joy and greatest privilege is to do justly and
to love mercy and to walk humbly with his God.
This, too, the story of Simon the Patriot tells us: not
what you were in the past, but, by the grace of God
what you are today, this is what counts! For the sake
of Him who died for us on Calvary, God forgives,
and forgets. He tells us, "I will remember your sins
no more!" Our sins forgiven and forgotten, we love
Him, and follow Him, and serve Him, in fervent
devotion. How can we possibly do less?

Just one thing more. Simon the Patriot was the
kind of man who could get excited. It is something
for which we pretend to be far too worldly-wise, far
too sophisticated today. It is so much more fashion-
able to appear bored. We must be calm and unemo-

tional. Don't ever let anyone know that you have come to faith in Jesus Christ, that you're all excited about your salvation, that inwardly you are leaping with joy because you are sharing in Christ's victory over sin and death and are living in the hope of heaven.

Wouldn't it be ever so much more fun to be a Christian if we could learn to catch the excitement that must have been felt by the Twelve as they lived out their discipleship with Jesus? And wouldn't we be better Christians and better citizens, too, if we weren't so terribly unconcerned about things and would really get excited enough about sin in our day and in our age to do something about it in the name and by the power and with the Gospel of Jesus Christ?

What are you and I really doing about the evils which are permitted to exist in our day, about the forces that are contributing to the mental and moral delinquency of our children, about the kind of thinking and living that is undermining the very foundations of our civilization, about the attitude which assumes that nothing is really sacred any more? Personal purity, marriage, the family, the home, the church—to millions of the people who share this planet with us these things are just a big joke. The worst of them let their hair grow, let their clothing become filthy, never take a bath, and call themselves beatniks. The more subtle, and therefore by far the more dangerous, are the people around us who, with a quiet contempt, or with a suave sophistication, simply ignore the old virtues, the qualities of character and the habits of life that mark and make the man, woman and child who walk in the ways of God.

Good old Dad—he hasn't gone to church for years. Brother and Sister haven't said a prayer or gone to communion since they went to college. Something's happened to Mother, she doesn't seem to care any more whether the children believe in God or not.

To many of the people in the community the church is either a nuisance or a convenience, never the divinely appointed agency to which the Lord Jesus Christ has entrusted the means of grace, the Word and the Sacraments, for the redemption of the lives and souls of men.

We need to get excited about these things. We who are supposed to be soldiers of Christ and subjects of His Kingdom, members, by grace, through faith, of His holy Church, what are we really doing to make the Church a living power in the community and the world, a power for the transformation of the individual, the improvement of society, the salvation of souls? What are we really doing to let God's Kingdom come besides talking to God about it in the Lord's Prayer? Are you going to leave it up to God? He says "It's up to you. I'll help. But it's up to you."

If we are doing only a little, or nothing at all, it's because we ourselves have not yet been changed as we ought to be changed, as we must be changed if we are to walk with God as disciples of Jesus Christ and begin to help change the world. It's because we ourselves have not yet been born again. Jesus once said, "Unless one is born anew, of water and the Spirit, he cannot enter the Kingdom of God." St. Paul, writing to the Romans, tells us, with an inspired play on words, "Do not be conformed to this world but be transformed by the renewal of your mind."

So Simon the Patriot became an apostle, a "special messenger" of Jesus Christ. So you and I can be born again, to walk with God, to serve the Lord Christ, to help in the building of His Kingdom, and, finally, to live with Him forever.

Judas is represented by a purse and thirty pieces of silver, the bribe he accepted to betray Jesus. Sometimes the emblem of Judas is totally blank indicating that the traitor deserves no remembrance.

Judas Iscariot

. . . . this ministry and apostleship from which Judas turned aside to go to his own place.

ACTS 1:25

JUDAS ISCARIOT

A traitor among the Twelve.

D O WE need an introduction to Judas Iscariot? He was one of the Twelve. The gospels make a point of that. It was Judas, they tell us, *"one of the Twelve,"* who betrayed Him.

This is the remarkable, the terrible thing, that the betrayal of Jesus was perpetrated by *"one of the Twelve!"*

It is clear that the story of Judas is one that has two principal chapters: what he was, and what he became.

After Judas was dead and gone, long after that night of horror and despair which ended with the ruptured body of Judas hanging from a tree near the dumping grounds of Jerusalem, Peter, also a fallen disciple, but now restored and called into apostleship, now the respected leader of the church in Jerusalem, reminded the faithful that someone ought to be elected to fill "this ministry and apostleship from which Judas turned aside to go to his own place." Phillips puts it this way, "that apostle's ministry which Judas forfeited to go where he belonged."

He was one of the Twelve. He was on his way to apostleship. But he went "to his own place." He went "where he belonged." The horrified judgment of a shocked and amazed humanity has followed him ever since.

A few friends and defenders Judas has had, and some of them quite sincere. They haven't all belonged to those "debunkers" of history who make a strange hobby of trying to prove that black is white and white is black, who tell us that George Washington and Abraham Lincoln were scoundrels and Napoleon was a great humanitarian. But the attempts to make a saint out of Judas have never quite succeeded. They've said that Judas, in all sincerity, was trying to force Jesus into a position in which He would have to flee from His enemies and save Himself or demonstrate His divine power and take over the world by force. They have pointed out that Judas, after all, when he realized what was going to happen as a result of the betrayal, was the only disciple who had courage enough to return and plead for the release of Jesus. But somehow it is terribly difficult to fit him out with a halo. He doesn't make a very good saint, and he is never pictured as one in the Bible. This isn't one of the forgotten disciples. Each of the four evangelists tells his story and tells it with broad hints of the shocked amazement it was bound to call forth in the hearts of all who would hear it and read it. After all, this was one of the Twelve.

Do you know what that meant? It meant that for

three years Judas lived and walked and talked with the Son of God. It was a privilege for which many today would gladly renounce all earthly possessions. To walk from dawn to starlight with Jesus of Nazareth, to sit at table with Him, to break bread with Him, to hear day in and day out the voice of Him who spoke as no one had ever spoken before, to follow Him who gave sight to the blind and hearing to the deaf, who stilled the storm and raised the dead, who, with a sweet gentleness, took little children into His arms and tenderly blessed them, who, with a holy anger and a righteous indignation, cleansed the temple of the racketeering money-changers, who spoke of sin and salvation, of divine judgment and divine forgiving love—these things were given to Judas just as they were given to all the rest, for he was one of the Twelve. There is no indication that he had become a disciple in any way different or unusual, with just this one possible exception: his name is followed by the word Iscariot, which scholars believe to mean that he was "a man of Kerioth," which was a village in southern Judea. In that case Judas Iscariot was the only one of the Twelve who did not come from Galilee, who did not share that northern homeland or speak with the Galilean accent. Does it matter, when we know that he shared, for three long and wonderful years, the intimate companionship of the Son of God? Does it matter, any more than it matters today whether you and I are of German, or Scandinavian, or southern European, or any other origin, so long as we have entered, by grace, through faith, into discipleship with Jesus Christ and belong to "the communion of saints"?

Think of what Judas, with such beginnings, with such wonderful advantages, might have become! The others, the faithful eleven, went on to noble service and merited fame, to the honor of a brave martyrdom and the everlasting rewards of heaven. In the liturgy of the church they are hailed as "the glorious company of the apostles." Cities, streets, churches, children, without number, have been called by their names. Above all, their names are written in the Book of Life. The very last thing the Bible has to say about Judas is that "he turned aside to go to his own place." He went "where he belonged." Judas could have become a minister of God and a great apostle of the Lord Jesus Christ. Instead, he is remembered as the perpetrator of the most despicable, the most shameful act in all the story of man. He didn't have to do it. Let's not blame God for it. Jesus knew that Judas would betray Him. But Jesus didn't make him do it. As long as Judas was with Jesus the door to forgiveness, the door to repentance, the door to a real and a true discipleship was always open. Let's not forget that. Let's not forget that this terrible thing happened to a man who was *one of the Twelve.*

Where do we stand today? Here we are in church, apparently believing disciples of the Lord Jesus Christ, come to hear His Word, to worship the eternal Father in the promised presence of His Son, to come before Him with praise and supplication, to present our tithes and offerings, to be strengthened in our most holy faith for an ever more faithful discipleship. Here we are, the most highly privileged people on all of God's earth, called into the Christian fellowship; forgiven, redeemed by the blood of Jesus Christ, shed for our sins on Calvary's Cross, cleansed, sanctified and destined to live forever; received, while we are still on earth, into the service of the everlasting King!

This is our story today. How will it end? You who are still so very young, the precious children whom the Savior so dearly loves; you older children and young adults, for whom the Master has many and wonderful plans; all of us, who call Him Lord and King and Redeemer, how will our story end? If it could happen to Judas, it can happen to you and me. We are all of us sinful, we are all of us sinners, we all have something of Judas within us.

So did the other disciples. But in their case the love of Jesus won out—the love with which He reached out to them and the loving response in their own hearts that brought them ever closer to Him. With Judas, somehow, it was different. The evil in Judas won out. As time went on the distance between them became greater and greater, until, at last, Judas, leaving the communion table in the Upper Room, went out into the darkness, into the darkness of a night from which he never returned. Let's pray to God that it won't ever happen to you or to me.

What *did* happen to Judas, anyway? Was it, after all, just that handful of coins, those thirty pieces of silver, worth about nineteen dollars and fifty cents? It is quite clear that money was a real problem with Judas. It would have been better for him had he made open confession of the fact that money came first in his life, that money had become his God, and, like the rich young man who wanted to follow Jesus but couldn't bring himself to part with his worldly possessions, had gone away and had never had any dealing with Jesus again. Then, at least, Judas would have been forgotten, as the rich young man has been forgotten. We don't even know his name. But the name of Judas is remembered with the most revolting act in history.

Jesus, of course, was quite aware of all this. One day He had spoken in mystical terms of Himself as the Bread and the Water of Life and had promised eternity itself to those who would eat His flesh and drink His blood. For many of His early followers it was just too much. This wasn't what they wanted to hear from the Messiah to whom they looked for the establishment of an earthly kingdom. St. John tells us that many of them, that day, "drew back and no longer went about with Him." Jesus turned to the Twelve with an almost pathetic and yet truly challenging question, "Will you also go away?" It was then that Simon Peter gave his magnificent answer, "Lord, to whom shall we go? You have the words of eternal life; and we have believed, and have come to know, that you are the Holy One of God." It must have brought great joy to the Master. Yet there was anguish in His soul. For Judas was still there, and Judas should have left with the rest. There is all the pathos of a breaking heart in His brief reply, "Did I not choose you, the Twelve, and one of you is a devil?"

Heaven help us, if ever Jesus finds it necessary to call us devils. It would be better for us never to have heard of Jesus at all. To know Him, and forsake Him, to be close to Him and betray Him is to place ourselves in danger of being consigned to the lowest hell! We may not like to hear it, but it's there, that "fearful prospect of judgment and a fury of fire," of which we are told in the tenth chapter of the letter to the Hebrews, the punishment of those who "sin deliberately after receiving the knowledge of the truth," the "much worse punishment . . . deserved by the man who has spurned the Son of God, and profaned the blood of the covenant by which he was sanctified, and outraged the Spirit of grace!" You and I may trifle with our religion from time to time, but there's nothing trivial about this as far as God is concerned. Even the ever-loving Jesus, kind and gentle, merciful and forgiving, called Judas, who was one of the Twelve, a devil, a "son of perdition." It must have hurt Him terribly, but He said it nevertheless. Judas was hell-bent for destruction. He was bound and determined to go his own way.

Just a few days before the betrayal Jesus was

resting in the house of Mary and Martha and Lazarus when Mary anointed her beloved Savior with a costly and fragrant ointment. Judas was incensed. "Why wasn't this sold," he snarled, "and the money given to the poor?" St. John tells us what he really had in mind, in the very next sentence. "This he said, not that he cared for the poor but because he was a thief, and as he had the money box he used to take what was put into it." Judas was the treasurer for Jesus and His disciples, and a crooked one, stealing from the meager funds that found their way into the common treasury. How often he had heard Jesus talking about money. It is said that one-sixth of the sayings of Jesus have something to say about money and the love of money and the fact that it is impossible to serve both God and Mammon. It meant very little to a man who was quietly stealing from the bag from which Jesus bought His daily bread. It meant nothing to a man who could contemplate selling the Son of God into the hands of His enemies for nineteen dollars and fifty cents!

In time, Judas may even have come to hate Jesus, to hate Him because He was opposed to everything that Judas loved. Jesus and everything that Jesus said and did were always getting in his way. Jesus was a continual embarrassment to him. Jesus troubled his conscience. Jesus unnerved him. For money was more important to Judas than anything else. It was a kind of disease with him, and when it suddenly became possible for him to get rid of Jesus and even make a little money at the same time, it was all he needed to plunge him into that black and terrible deed. Money was Judas' passport to hell.

Look into your own life and make your own applications. You know, far better than anyone else outside of the Lord Himself, just where you stand. Write your own sermon and preach it to yourself. You can do it far better than I can.

Remember, there's a passport to heaven, too, the forgiving mercy and redeeming love of God the Father through Jesus Christ, His Son. Judas "turned aside to go to his own place." He went "where he belonged." Since Jesus died for us, we belong to God, and the *place* where we belong is on the road that leads to heaven.

A carpenter's square and a spear are ascribed to Thomas because he is said to have erected with his own hands a church at Malipar, in India, later suffering death by martyrdom.

Thomas

Thomas, called the Twin, said to his fellow disciples, "Let us also go, that we may die with him."

JOHN 11:16

Thomas said to him, "Lord, we do not know where you are going; how can we know the way?"

JOHN 14:5

Thomas answered him, "My Lord and my God!"

JOHN 20:28

THOMAS

His doubting mind found its answer.

ISN'T it true that often, when we really get to know people, we think of them quite differently than we did before?

This is exactly what happens when we really get to know Thomas. People have been calling him "Doubting Thomas" for who knows how many years. Ask someone what he knows about Thomas and he will probably say, "You mean the disciple who refused to believe that Jesus had risen from the dead. All I know is that the world has been calling him 'Doubting Thomas' ever since." Thomas has a kind of shady reputation. Like Judas he has stood for centuries in the shadows of the world's contempt.

We have tried to understand Judas Iscariot. All kinds of attempts have been made to explain away the shamefulness of his betrayal. In the light of the Bible record and the awful judgment of Christ Himself, those attempts have failed. There is no condemnation of Thomas in the Bible. There is no indication that Jesus was offended by his questions. Thomas deserves to be taken out of the shadows of

the world's contempt into the light of a true understanding, a real appreciation of his character.

Of course he had a questioning mind. Don't you?
Of course he had doubts from time to time. Don't
you? But the Bible doesn't call him "Doubting
Thomas." Maybe you do, but the Bible doesn't. The
gospel writers introduce him to us as Thomas or
Didymus, and both of those words mean simply "The
Twin." Possibly it wasn't even a name in those days,
just a nickname. They called him "The Twin." I
like to think that the others used this name affec-
tionately, just as you and I feel particularly close to
people whom we call by a familiar nickname. I like
to think that they loved him, which is more than
we can say for Judas. I know that Jesus loved him.
Judas was an evil man. Thomas was apparently an
intelligent individual, with a probing, searching
mind, restless at times and deeply troubled, but only
because he was so eager in the quest for truth. I am
terribly grateful that there was a Thomas among
the Twelve, for there are so many people like him
today. Thomas is proof to all the world that the questioning, probing, even doubting mind can find its
answers in the living Christ.

We don't know who he was or where he came
from. We know nothing about the individual, man
or woman, to whom he was a twin. While the other
evangelists only mention his name, it is St. John who
unfolds the drama of Thomas for us, a drama in three
acts, of which the world, with a strange preoccupa-

tion, has remembered only the third and largely forgotten the other two.

The first act of the drama, believe me, is one to be remembered. It should never have been forgotten, for it tells us something about Thomas, which, by comparison, may well put us all to shame.

Already the brief ministry of Jesus is drawing to a close. He has become immensely popular. The people to whom He has spoken and to whom He has ministered dearly love Him. Many of them are quietly hoping and planning to make Him their king. In Jerusalem, on the other hand, a lethal hatred is building up against Him. The leaders of church and state are determined to do away with Him. His disciples are very much aware of all this. It was all so evident the last time they had been in Jerusalem, and they had been so relieved when, at last, He had returned to the comparative safety of the land beyond Jordan. Suddenly a message comes from Bethany. His dear friend Lazarus, brother of Mary and Martha, is ill. For two days Jesus waits, then He announces, "We are going back to Judea." A storm of opposition greets Him. They tell Him of the hatred of the priests and Pharisees and of their announced intention of putting Him to death. Jesus doesn't seem to hear them. Quietly He says to them, "Our friend Lazarus has fallen asleep, but I go to awake him out of sleep." Characteristically, the disciples don't understand. "Lord," they say to Him, "if he has fallen asleep, he will recover." Sleep is good for a patient. He must be getting better. Then Jesus speaks to them in their own language, and says to them plainly, "Lazarus is dead; and for your sake I am glad that I was not there, so that you may believe. But let us go to him." And now Thomas speaks, whom so many have held in contempt, and this is what he says, "Let us also go, that we may die with Him."

Had Simon Peter said it, we wouldn't be at all surprised. Peter was always making brash declarations, and sometimes they turned out to be utterly magnificent, like this proposal which came, not from Peter, but from Thomas. It may be the first time you have met this particular Thomas. I'm sure you think much more kindly of him, knowing that it was he who said, "Let us also go that we may die with Him."

Thomas did die a martyr's death, not that week in Jerusalem, but many years later, after fruitful missionary labors in far-off India. The Thomas legend is strong in the history of India. Thomas Churches, Thomas Christians, innumerable relics of his living and dying there are still to be found. He whom the world remembers for his great doubt has been, instead, a lamp of divine truth, a blazing torch, kindling, in the darkness of pagan India and in the hearts of its benighted millions, the first flickering flames of the Christian faith. Courage, loyalty, love, these are the qualities of the Thomas whom we meet today. While the others loudly plead with Jesus to save His own skin, thinking perhaps of their own safety, too,

Thomas brushes all their fears aside and says, "If this is what the Master wants, if this is what He must do, what are we arguing about? What does it matter, even if we die with Him?"

When I see, with something of a sickened sensation in the pit of my stomach, what Christianity amounts to in the lives of so many today, I wonder, sometimes, how many of us would say it: "Let us also go, that we may die with Him." We know so much more than Thomas knew at that moment. We have been to Calvary and we've looked up at the Cross, and we have heard the Father saying in His Word, "He died for you. For His sake I will forgive your sins and forget them. He died so that you may live forever." We know that this was all part of God's plan for our eternal redemption. We know it and we profess to believe it, and yet, how many of us, how many of the millions who clutter up the membership lists of Christian churches, would say, "I'm willing to go and die with Him"? How many of us would be willing to follow Him to the Cross? How many of us would be in church on a Sunday morning, how many of us would claim discipleship with Him, if a totalitarian government, bent on erasing religion from the life of the nation, had decreed, "You shall worship this Christ no more, on pain of death"? It was Thomas, whom most Christians have always regarded with a degree of contempt, who proposed to the other disciples, whom we have always held in much higher regard, "Let us also go, that we may die with Him."

Thomas was ready to die with Him, when many "Christians" today aren't even willing to live with Him, except in certain very restricted areas of their lives. They may be Sunday morning Christians, or Christmas and Easter Christians, but they are very definite about the fact that Christ has nothing to say about their business or their entertainment. They may tell you in just so many words, "I never let religion interfere with my private life." Some of us, a good deal closer to Christ, think of ourselves as just a little lower than the angels and very nearly saints, when we put a couple of dollars into a church offering envelope or attend services more than once a week. I wonder how many of us are really capable of a discipleship that goes all the way. Thomas was willing even to die with Christ. Later on he did.

Act two of the Thomas story finds the disciples with Jesus in the Upper Room. The Master is telling them that He is going away. "Let not your hearts be troubled"; the quiet, tender voice is saying, "believe in God, believe also in Me. In My Father's house are many rooms; if it were not so, would I have told you that I go to prepare a place for you? . . . And you know the way where I am going." But Thomas could contain himself no longer. It was all so terribly sad and solemn, so completely bewildering. "Lord," he cried, "we do not know where you

are going; how can we know the way?" It was then
that Jesus said to Thomas and to them all, yearning
to dispel for them the darkness in which they were
helplessly groping, "I am the way, and the truth, and
the life; no one comes to the Father, but by Me."

Christ is still the answer, and the only answer,
even today. Your doubting, probing, questioning
mind is likely to say, "Why that's ridiculous! It
doesn't make sense! So often I feel like one who is
lost in the dark. So often I wonder with Pilate, 'What
is truth!' So often I see nothing in the future, nothing
I can be really sure of but inevitable death. You tell
me that you know the answer. You come whispering
a name. Jesus, the Christ. You're out of your mind.
You're one of those religious fanatics. You don't know
what you are talking about!"

There's only one reply to that. Try it and see.
Open your heart to this Jesus, the Christ of the Holy
Scripture, open your life to Him and let Him enter
it with all His wonderful wisdom, with all His wonderful love. Meet Him face to face as Son of God
and Savior of men and accept Him as your own.
Count on Him, count on Him for everything, trust
above all in the everlasting benefits of His redeeming sacrifice on Calvary's Cross, and you will know,
and what blessed knowledge it is, that He *is* the way
and the truth and the life! He will become to you
Alpha and Omega, the beginning and the end, your
All-In-All. You can thank Thomas for asking a searching question. You can thank Jesus for a completely

satisfactory answer. The next time you feel lost in the dark, the next time you feel bewildered by life's problems, the next time you are gloomy and depressed, say to yourself, "What would Jesus say? What *did* He say?" or "What would Jesus do? What *did* He do?" For Christ is the answer, the way, the truth, the life!

The third act takes us to the golden days of the week after Easter, radiant, wonderful, joyous days for those who had seen the risen Lord, but dark days for Thomas, for he had not been there with the rest. He had seen how Jesus died. To believe now that He was suddenly and gloriously alive—it was too much for Thomas, still in a state of mental and spiritual shock. "I must see Him for myself," he said. Can we blame him? Would we have been any more inclined to believe? Aren't we always wondering, questioning, doubting today?

A week later Jesus appeared to them again, and this time Thomas was with them. "The doors were shut," St. John tells us, "but Jesus came and stood among them, and said, 'Peace be with you.'" The eyes of Jesus were searching for Thomas. "Thomas," He said, "put your finger here, and see my hands; and put out your hand, and place it in my side; do not be faithless, but believing." Thomas had been looking for evidence. Here it was, in overwhelming reality. Almost before the gentle voice had finished speaking, Thomas was on his knees, at the nail-pierced feet, saying, "My Lord and my God!" It was all he could say, but it was enough. This was worship, the worship of a once doubting but now believing disciple, and it was gratefully and graciously accepted by the risen Lord. Then, from Jesus, came a gentle reproach. "Have you believed because you have seen Me? Blessed are those who have not seen and yet believe."

If you and I believe in Him today, then Jesus was talking, in that moment, about you and me. For we have not seen Him as Thomas did. By faith, by God's great gift of a wonderful faith, we are aware of His living presence. We know Him as Lord and God and everlasting Redeemer.

"Blessed," Jesus says, "happy are those who have not seen and yet believe." To such blessed, happy believers St. Peter writes, "Without having seen Him you love Him; though you do not now see Him you believe in Him and rejoice with unutterable and exalted joy. As the outcome of your faith you obtain the salvation of your souls."

Crossed keys indicate the charge given to Peter on the basis of his great confession.

Peter

> *Jesus looked at him, and said, "So you are Simon, the son of John? You shall be called Cephas" (which means Peter).**
>
> JOHN 1:42

---

*Footnote in the Revised Standard Version: From the word for *rock* in Aramaic and Greek, respectively.

PETER

A man of clay who became a rock.

IT WAS a sunny Sunday morning in early November. Full of that sense of wonder and unreality that comes to you when something you have been thinking about and reading about for years and years actually happens to you, I found myself approaching St. Peter's Cathedral in Rome. There it was, the colonnaded square and the obelisk, the horse carts, the statues, the great dome flanked by the Vatican palaces, the vast doors, and people, people everywhere, streaming in and out of that almost unbelievably huge and magnificent church, priests, monks, nuns, seminarians, all in their characteristic garb, a few camera-toting off-season tourists like myself and my Air Force son, and the faithful of Rome, making their pilgrimages.

Once inside, we saw at once the famed statue of the apostle for whom the cathedral is named. No rough and tumble fisherman is pictured here. It is a bearded dignitary cast in bronze and bedecked with all the trappings of a pope, including a great jewelled crown. How often I had wondered if it was really true that people came and kissed the bronze toe of the statue as they passed it, had kissed it so often, in fact, in the course of the years, that from time to time it has been worn away and has had to be replaced. There it was, and the people, in endless procession, were kissing the toe, some with great reverence, some very quickly, some, usually the better dressed men and women, only after wiping it carefully with a handkerchief. There were mothers and fathers holding up their children, even babies, so that their little lips might touch the sacred extremity.

I wondered what Peter would say of all this. What would Peter, the Peter whom I have learned to know in the gospels, say of this city, this "Babylon," as he called it, to which he had come with the story of the crucified and risen Christ, this proud and ancient Rome to which he had brought the message of the Cross, in whose deep, damp, dark and dusty catacombs he had broken the bread of life, in whose dungeons he had been imprisoned and where, apparently, he died, crucified, the legend tells us, not like his Lord and Master, but upside-down? What would Peter say of this modern Rome, this cathedral, and five hundred lesser churches, this statue, these people? I'm not going to try to answer that. Peter was a very colorful, impetuous, outspoken individual. I would love to know what Peter would say about modern Rome and St. Peter's Cathedral and the statue of himself and the things that are happening there. I can only tell you what my impression was. The Simon Peter I knew wasn't there.

He's in the gospels. He lives for us in the vivid pages of the inspired Scripture. He's there, vibrantly alive and intensely human. It is a character portrait presented to us in fascinating detail. We learn to know him far better than any of the others among the Twelve. "The Big Fisherman" he has often been called, the man of the rugged physique, the great, strong body, the rough, hard hands, accustomed to hauling dripping nets out of Galilee and sailing a fishing boat on stormy seas, with a voice and a personality to go with it, the big fisherman who became, at the Lord's command, a fisher of men. In some ways the weakest of Christ's disciples, he was in many ways the strongest, too, and, of the Twelve, became His greatest apostle. We shudder at some of the things he said, and admire him for others. We are amazed at his denial. Yet we love him today as one of the noblest of them all.

Do we love him so because of his weaknesses, because the very foibles and failings and foolishnesses of his character tell us that there is hope even for us? We had better look into that and remember that Peter is great and beloved not because of what he was when Jesus met him, but because of what he became under the influence of Christ, molded, like clay in the hands of a master potter, into a vessel of rugged beauty, of great strength, of wonderful practical usefulness.

It all began that day when Andrew had come home, all excited, shouting that he had found the Messiah. We don't know what Peter replied to that amazing announcement of his brother. St. John reports simply, "He brought him to Jesus." There is just a hint in those words that Peter had to be dragged a little. After all, it was late in the day and this was a preposterous assumption. But Peter went along, and soon he was looking into the eyes of Jesus. Jesus, looking at Peter, said, "So you are Simon, the son of John? You shall be called Cephas."

Today the words of Jesus would sound like this: "So you're Simon Johnson! I'm going to call you 'The Rock!' "

One day, long months later, Jesus said to His disciples, "What are they saying about Me out there?" They answered, "Some say that you are John the Baptist come back to life; others say Elijah, or Jeremiah, or some other prophet." Quietly Jesus asked, "What do *you* think?"

It was Peter who answered, Peter, the self-appointed "speaker of the house" who so often spoke up for the rest. "You are the Messiah," he said, "the Son of the living God!" And Jesus said to him, "Blessed are you, Simon Johnson, for flesh and blood has not revealed this to you, but My Father who is in heaven. And I tell you, you are Peter (The Rock) and on this rock I will build My church, and the gates of hell shall not prevail against it. I will give you the keys of the kingdom of heaven, and whatever you bind on earth shall be bound in heaven, and whatever you loose on earth shall be loosed in heaven."

It was a promise and a power which, on Easter afternoon, was bestowed by a risen Savior upon the others, too. "Receive the Holy Spirit," He said to them all. "If you forgive the sins of any, they are forgiven; if you retain the sins of any, they are retained."

Peter had come a long way. He had learned a great deal. Jesus, the prophet of Nazareth, had become for him Son of God and promised Redeemer, even before His awful death and glorious resurrection, and Peter's marvellous confession of faith became for Christ the rock foundation on which, He said, He would build His church.

Ever since, we who have shared that faith and that confession, and *all* who have shared it, have been part of His church, one holy fellowship, one blessed communion of saints. When we follow Him, as Peter did, when we believe in Him, as Peter did, when we count on Him, as Peter did, for life and salvation, then into our hands, too, He presses the keys of the kingdom of heaven. Sin, death and hell, all have been vanquished in Him who lived and died for us and rose again for our justification. We are going to live forever. In the fellowship of His believing church we are able to comfort one another with these words.

It didn't mean that Peter, having made his wonderful confession of faith, was ready now for graduation from Christ's training school, the perfect disciple, the unblemished saint. It was just a short time later that he earned from Jesus a terrible rebuke. Jesus had been telling them that He must return to Jerusalem, to suffer there at the hands of His enemies, and to die.

This is the story as St. Matthew tells it: "And Peter took Him and began to rebuke Him, saying, 'God forbid, Lord! This shall never happen to you.' But He turned and said to Peter, 'Get behind Me, Satan! You are a hindrance to Me; for you are not on the side of God, but of men.' "

What was Peter's sin? He was arguing with the purposes of God. He had dared to stand in the way when Jesus was about to begin the final stages of His journey to the cross. When you do that, Jesus said, you are on Satan's side and stand with sinful men.

Speaking now to them all, Jesus said, "If any man would come after Me, let him deny himself and take up his cross and follow Me. For whoever would save his life will lose it, and whoever loses his life for My sake will find it."

How often, like Peter, haven't we thought that other things were more important than the things that God has in store for those who follow in the footsteps of Christ? How reluctantly and with what eloquent complaints we deny ourselves and make a pretext of taking up the cross to follow Him! How little of life and the things of life, our time, our talents, our treasure, we are willing to sacrifice for Him! Some people we know have not been willing at all. Trying to *keep* it all for themselves, life and the things of life, they've *lost* it all. They've gone to death and damnation unsaved. Others, laying their lives at His feet, willing to give it all up for Him, willing to bear His cross, or whatever cross He lays upon them, have *found* life, have found *eternal* life in Him!

Someone has said that Simon Peter was consistently inconsistent. He was always going from the heights to the depths and back again. There was that stormy day on Lake Galilee when he had courage enough and faith enough even to walk on the water toward his welcoming Lord. Suddenly, finding himself beyond the safety of the boat, terrified by wind and wave, he became afraid and sank, crying, "Lord, save me," as he grasped the Master's helping hand. Consistently inconsistent, that was Peter's discipleship.

In the Upper Room on Maundy Thursday Peter didn't want Jesus to wash his feet. A moment later he said, "Not my feet only, but also my hands and my head!" That night he solemnly assured his Lord that he would die with Him before he would forsake Him. A few hours later he was trying to prove, by cursing like a godless fisherman, that he had never heard of Jesus. In the Garden he slashed about with a sword, playing the big hero, ready to fight the whole army single-handed. A moment later he ran away. Consistently inconsistent!

How quickly we fault him for it, and forget the strange and terrible inconsistencies of our own discipleship. One moment we are deeply religious; the next, God seems a million miles away. One moment our faith is strong and wholesome; the next it is riddled with questions and honeycombed with doubts and fears. One moment we love this Savior of ours with all our hearts; the next we hear ourselves denying Him, ashamed to have a part in Him.

Or we do this. We hear a sermon, we read something in the Bible, we think about all the good Christians in the world, and we make up our minds to be better Christians ourselves, and then we forget our good resolutions almost as soon as we leave the church or close the book. We are troubled in conscience by the fact that we go to church irregularly and receive the holy sacrament just once in a great while, and we tell ourselves that we ought to be doing much better, but we don't. When we do come, we kneel with our fellow Christians in the house of God, some of us on very unaccustomed knees, and confess our sins, saying to our heavenly Father, "I am heartily sorry for them and sincerely repent of them, and sincerely and earnestly purpose, by the assistance of God the Holy Ghost, henceforth to amend my sinful life," and then we go home and go on living just as we did before. We say to our Father in heaven, "Forgive us our trespasses as we forgive those who trespass against us," and the next day we are just as mean and irritable, just as uncharitable

and unforgiving as we have always been. Consistently inconsistent. That's our discipleship, too.

The wonderful thing about Peter is that he did
experience at last a complete transformation. The
man of clay became a rock. It meant months of
being hammered and pounded on the anvils of
God. It meant months of being molded by a mercy
such as only the Son of God would apply to such
a man. No matter what Peter said or did, no
matter how foolish it was or how noble and brave
and good, the love of Jesus was always there, prais-
ing him when he deserved to be praised, scolding him
sternly when he needed the discipline of a strong
rebuke, warning him in the face of danger, saving
him always when he needed to be saved.

In the courtyard of Peter's awful denial it was a
long, searching look that pierced him to the depths
of his soul. On Easter morning it was the message of
the angel to the women at the empty tomb, "Go tell
His disciples and Peter." Don't forget Peter; he needs
it even more than the others. That day Jesus appeared to Peter alone. We have never been told what
transpired between them. He saw the Lord again
that afternoon, when Thomas was absent and a week
later, when Thomas was there and believed. Then,
days later, they were back in Galilee, back at the
old business of fishing, and He appeared to them
once more, and they ate with Him at dawn on the
beach. That morning Jesus said to Peter, "Simon, son
of John, do you love me?" Three times the question

came and three times the tortured answer of the
fallen disciple, "Lord, you know that I do!" Three
times the risen Savior said it, "Feed My lambs. Feed
My lambs. Tend My sheep!" And, finally, "You will
serve Me, Peter, and you will die for Me. Follow
Me."

Soon it was Pentecost, and the promises of the
ascended Savior were fulfilled in the gift of the Holy
Spirit. Now there was nothing in all the world that
could shake the rock that was Peter and the rock
that was Peter's faith. With one fearless and utterly
magnificent sermon he brought three thousand converts into the infant church. They had sensed the
flaming power of the Spirit. They heard the message
of Him who was crucified and had risen again.

This is the story of what happened: "Now when
they heard this they were cut to the heart, and said
to Peter and the rest of the apostles, 'Brethren, what
shall we do? And Peter said to them, 'Repent, and be
baptized every one of you in the name of Jesus
Christ for the forgiveness of your sins . . .' . . . So
those who received his word were baptized and there
were added that day about three thousand souls.
And they devoted themselves to the apostles' teach-
ing and fellowship, to the breaking of bread and the
prayers."

Peter grew old in the service of his Redeemer and
great in the service of the church. Caligula, Claudius,
Nero, followed each other on the throne of imperial
Rome; waves of persecution swept across the Chris-

tian fellowship; fleeing believers scattered the seeds of the faith wherever they went; even in death by martyrdom they gained converts for the eternal kingdom.

Peter wrote to them, strengthening them in their fiery trials, reminding them that they had been "born anew to a living hope through the resurrection of Jesus Christ from the dead, and to an inheritance which is imperishable, undefiled, and unfading, kept in heaven for you, who by God's power are guarded through faith for a salvation ready to be revealed in the last time."

"After you have suffered a while," he wrote to them, "the God of all grace, who has called you to His eternal glory in Christ, will Himself restore, establish, strengthen you."

How well he knew. Hadn't it happened to him? Wasn't that Peter's own story, from beginning to end?

Let it be your story, too, and mine.